SPECIAL
TEACHING
IN HIGHER EDUCATION

SPECIAL TEACHING

IN HIGHER EDUCATION

Successful strategies for access and inclusion

edited by

Stuart Powell

KOGAN PAGE

London and Sterling, VA

First published in Great Britain and the United States in 2003 by Kogan Page Limited

120 Pentonville Road
London N1 9JN
UK
www.kogan-page.co.uk

22883 Quicksilver Drive
Sterling VA 20166-2012
USA

ISBN   0 7494 3610 7 (hbk)
        0 7494 3611 5 (pbk)

British Library Cataloguing-in-Publication Data

A CIP record for this book is available from the British Library.

Library of Congress Cataloging-in-Publication Data
Special teaching in higher education : successful strategies for access and inclusion / edited by Stuart Powell.
    p. cm.
Includes bibliographical references and index.
  ISBN 0-7494-3610-7 – ISBN 0-7494-3611-5 (pbk.)
  1. People with disabilities–Education (Higher)–Great Britain. 2.
College students with disabilities–Great Britain. 3. Special
education–Great Britain. 4. Inclusive education–Great Britain. I.
Powell, Stuart.
  LC4814. G72S369 2003
  371.9'0474'0941–dc21
                            2002154767

Typeset by Jean Cussons Typesetting, Diss, Norfolk
Printed and bound in Great Britain by Clays Ltd, St Ives plc

Dedication

In memory of my father who died during my work on this book

Contents

Contributing authors

Jeremy Cooper is a barrister and Professor of Law at Middlesex University, where he heads the Disability Law and Policy Research Unit. He has written widely on comparative disability issues, and is the editor of *Law, Rights and Disability*, published in 2000 by Jessica Kingsley.

Martyn Cooper, by background a systems engineer, has been working in the area of technology for disabled people for the past 15 years. He heads the Accessible Educational Media (AEM) group at the Open University, UK. As well as researching accessibility approaches and issues of access for disabled students to electronic media he has a key role in enabling the OU to meet the needs of its 8,000 disabled students.

Stella Cottrell is currently working as a Full Time Inspector for the Adult Learning Inspectorate. Previously she spent over 10 years in higher education, working in learning development and teaching and learning. She has been a consultant to over 20 universities on issues of dyslexia support, and was a member of the HEFCE-funded National Working Party on Dyslexia in Higher Education. Her publications include *The Study Skills Handbook* (Palgrave, 1999) and *Teaching Study Skills and Supporting Learning* (Palgrave, 2001).

Mary Davies is the Study Support and Dyslexia Support Tutor at Swansea Institute of Higher Education. Her main role is to support students in their learning through individual and group study skills programmes and through study skills modules delivered in-house. She has an academic background in English literature, and her current research interest is in the link between students' learning styles and their study skills needs.

Christopher Hopkins is currently part-time Student Advisor with the Disabilities and Additional Needs Service at Loughborough University. In addition, he is a freelance disability consultant and trainer and is qualified to provide both disability equality training and access auditing. Christopher has an MA in Disability Studies from the University of Leeds. He is a disabled person having been born with spina bifida and hydrocephalus.

Joy Jarvis is a teacher of the deaf who has worked in a range of contexts with deaf children and adults. She is currently responsible for training teachers of the deaf at the University of Hertfordshire. Her publications are in the field of deaf education, particularly in relation to issues of inclusion.

Caralinda Jefferies is the Learning and Teaching Support Tutor at Swansea Institute of Higher Education. Her duties include responsibility for coordinating the development of the Institute's Learning and Teaching Strategy. Formerly a lecturer in computing, she has an interest in developments in computer based learning in higher education.

Professor Alan V Jones was a Head of the Department of Chemistry and Physics at Nottingham Trent University and also a teacher trainer. His interest in pupils and students with disabilities has ranged over almost 30 years and has resulted in many publications (books and articles) for school and university use. Although recently retired he still conducts courses in the areas of science and special needs for schools, LEAs, conferences and universities, in the United Kingdom and overseas.

Pamela Knight is an experienced teacher of the deaf who was previously course leader of the Advanced Diploma in the Education of Deaf Children at the University of Leeds. She has published in the field of deaf education and is currently involved in the inspection of courses in higher education.

Dr Tim Luckett currently teaches English to students at Zhejiang Wanli University, Ningbo, China. During his time at the University of Hertfordshire, he worked on a number of autism-related research projects, each of which examined a different aspect of education in practice.

Dr Tim Parke teaches linguistics and education at the University of Hertfordshire. He has experience of several sectors of education, including programmes for the British Council, and has worked with English language teachers on advanced training and MA courses in the UK and overseas.

Professor Stuart Powell is Director of Research Degrees at the University of Hertfordshire. He has researched and published widely in the area of educational psychology, and in particular around issues of critical thinking and special educational needs. His current post enables him to focus on quality issues related to teaching and learning in higher education.

Dr Archie W N Roy is Post-16 Education Officer for RNIB Scotland and is based at the Centre for Sensory Impaired People in Glasgow. He trained in developmental psychology, and publishes widely on issues such as transition into employment by visually impaired students and the effects of sight loss on self-perception.

James Wade is Senior Officer, Young People's Project, for Rethink: Severe Mental Illness (formerly known as NSF, the National Schizophrenia Fellowship). His work has included mental health promotion in the student community, a national conference examining suicide issues and students' vulnerability, and development of @ease, a mental health Web site resource for young people. He has worked in the voluntary sector for four years since graduating in his late 20s.

Preface

The education system in the UK has focused increasingly on provision of a 'curriculum for all'. Certainly in the school-age sector, access to education is clearly established as an entitlement for all individuals, and increasingly it is deemed appropriate that that education should be delivered within the mainstream context. Whatever the success of particular policies and procedures in these respects, it is clear that students are now gaining access to education where in the recent past they would have been excluded. In some areas (such as hearing impairment) ideological and methodological advances have been aided by technological advances (like the use of 'phonic ear' systems). In short, the potential of many students is now being realized to a greater extent than ever before. This phenomenon has progressed naturally from the school sector into FE and now HE.

This book addresses the learning needs of students within identified populations, and suggests effective responses of the staff in designing and delivering the curriculum. It offers discussion of teaching strategies that provide flexibility with regard to distinctive modes of learning, with individual chapters offering insights into how individuals may learn in special ways. Contributing authors cover the whole of the student experience, thus including social dimensions along with issues of academic learning.

Underpinning the book is the notion that higher education requires a level of critical thinking on the part of all students, and that there is therefore a need for all concerned to look beyond any particular disability or difficulty to the potential of students to learn to think with clarity and critical awareness within their chosen discipline. The text offers an analysis of the relationship between learning and teaching within HE, and the particular learning needs of some students. In this sense it examines the pedagogy of HE from particular perspectives within it. At the end of each of the parts of the book dealing with direct teaching, themes and issues are drawn together in short chapters.

It should be stressed here that the book is about special teaching: a liberal interpretation is therefore made of what situations might require that teaching. The topics within the book are not limited to areas that might commonly be known as 'special needs'. For example, there is a chapter on students for whom English is a second language, suggesting not that they have special needs in the traditional sense of the term, but rather that they require special teaching if they are to be successful. The book, then, goes beyond narrow interpretations of disabled, learning difficulties and special needs.

List of abbreviations

ADA	Americans with Disabilities Act (United States)
ADP	Association of Disabled Professionals
AS	Asperger's syndrome
ASD	autistic spectrum disorder(s)
BDA	British Dyslexia Association
CAA	computer aided assessment
C&IT	communications and information technology
DDA	Disability Discrimination Act
DSA	Disabled Students Award
DEYTA	Federal Department for Education, Training and Youth Affairs (Australia)
HE	higher education
HEI	higher educational institution
HFA	high-functioning autism
HREOC	Human Rights and Equal Opportunities Commission (Australia)
IDEA	Individuals with Disabilities Education Act (United States)
IEP	Individualized Education Programme (United States)
IT	information technology
LMS	learning management system
MLE	managed learning environment
QAA	Quality Assurance Agency
RNIB	Royal National Institute for the Blind
SENDA	Special Needs and Disability Act (2001)
SHEFC	Scottish Higher Education Funding Council
SpLDs	special learning difficulties
VLE	virtual learning environment
W3C	World Wide Web Consortium
WAI	Web Accessibility Initiative

Part one

Introduction

1

Special teaching in higher education

Stuart Powell

Introduction

This chapter seeks to outline the approach taken in the book and indicate its underlying principles. The genesis of the book is described by way of giving an initial justification, and subsequently the way it is structured around identified areas, deemed to require special teaching, is discussed. The issue of the right for all to be able to access appropriate education is explored, along with the needs for a new kind of curricular flexibility and openness in higher education. Finally, the chapter emphasizes the valuing of diversity, and the need to recognize and understand the range of individual differences in learning, and respond to them with a way of teaching that utilizes knowledge of special skills and strategies.

Origins

The origins of this book can be traced to two complementary sources. Some of my own professional work involves issues surrounding autism, and the psychology and education of individuals with 'autistic spectrum disorders' (ASD). Much of the pioneering research and practice in the field has been targeted at the early years, the years of formal schooling, and care in the post-schooling phase. But as understanding of autism and its range of manifestations across the spectrum (and I include here Asperger's syndrome) has improved, as diagnosis has become more sophisticated and more widely available, and as provision within the school sector has increased, so the issues have been pushed up the age range. Individuals who less than 20 years ago would have been described by those in authority as mystifyingly odd, and who would have had little formal schooling of an appropriate kind, and therefore little opportunity of progressing into further or higher education, are now gaining an appropriate education. Consequently they are proving themselves able to gain access to higher education, and potentially to be successful within it. Of course this success story brings with it new challenges for all concerned. I have been contacted on a number of occasions by parents of young people with autism about to go to university, anxious to know what can be done to facilitate their child's successful inclusion within that university. Similarly, I have been contacted by lecturers who either have or are about to have a student in their classes with a diagnosis of ASD, and who want to know at a very pragmatic level what they should do to enable that student to be successful.

I should note that anxiety often typifies both parents and professionals, though clearly the roots of that anxiety are different. Parents have invariably had the child's lifetime of experience of trying to understand him or her, trying to pass on their understanding to professionals, and also often to persuade professionals of the child's needs and potential. This is not the place to go into the detail surrounding understanding of autism, but it is important perhaps to note that parents are often experts on their own child, though not necessarily expert in the complexities of educational systems. The anxiety of lecturers often relates to their own lack of knowledge about the condition and its relationships to the kind of learning that goes on in university, and sometimes to a worry about the effects on the other students of the individual's presence in learning groups and within the cohort as a whole. My premise is that anxiety is a natural enough state of mind in this respect, and that those willing to ask the questions, as long as they are asking with a view to improving their own teaching, have made the necessary first step to success. (I am making this premise even if some of the initial questions and the attitudes that underpin them are misguided in themselves.) What is really required of educators, at least in the first instance, is a willingness to try to understand; the pragmatics leading to successful inclusion for the individual student will follow.

The second source of this book is a more personal one, and I note it here merely to indicate why I think it is so important to recognize that some students have needs that are special, and yet also amenable to resolution. My daughter progressed through the school system successfully because key individual teachers and headteachers were prepared to take on ideas and procedures with which they were wholly unfamiliar. Her profound hearing loss was a challenge to her and to those she came into contact with. (I recognize here that the issues are not just matters of 'challenge' – see the section on Diversity later in this chapter.) At the stage of university entrance, a new set of challenges faced all concerned. Again, it was the willingness of key academic staff to set their minds to how to enable her very specific needs to be met that was a key factor in her ultimate success in degree-level work. This is not, of course, to underplay her own determination and ability. In the period during which this phase of her education was taking place, there was little published material to help academic and support staff in their efforts. The intention behind this book is that academics in similar positions today will find explanation and guidance in particular chapters – in the instance quoted here, in the chapter by Jarvis and Knight (Chapter 4).

Structure of this book
A fragmented view of pedagogical issues?

Some readers may find the approach taken in this book unusual in the current climate of special needs provision in society in general, and in education in particular. Indeed, some may share the discomfort felt by an academic colleague, who rejected involvement with the book on the grounds, one, that the approach taken 'suggests a somewhat fragmented view of pedagogical issues associated with access and disability', and two, that a more appropriate approach would be to 'address the pedagogy first and look at how it might be adapted, by means of dialogue, to fit the needs of individual students. In other words, to determine the learning needs of the student body as a whole and then to design a curriculum that, as far as possible, takes account of the heterogeneity of learning needs.' In putting forward these criticisms the argument is made that the approach taken in the book runs counter to 'a more inclusive approach'. I take the liberty of repeating the discomforts expressed here because I think they represent in broad terms a body of opinion that needs recognition. I am not merely trying to create a straw man or woman, but rather to recognize a view (and one that may dominate thinking in this area at the moment).

Inherent in the criticisms outlined above is a reluctance to see individuals as having definable and special needs with regard to their education, that can be directly addressed in a compartmentalized way. For some, to have chapters specifically addressing the needs, for example, of the hearing impaired is to run the risk of returning to the days when individuals with such needs were separated out by their disability and offered something different by way of education: a different curriculum delivered in a different way and in a different location.

Does the structure of the book, then, suggest a fragmented view of pedagogical issues associated with access and disability? Clearly it suggests that it is reasonable to separate out different kinds of disability and specific learning need, in respect of at least some aspects of the educative process. In so doing it does not deny in my view that there are some commonalities in terms of issues – indeed these are picked up in the 'Issues for pedagogy' chapters. For example, it does not suggest denial of the principle of equal right of access to the possibility of success in education. But it does suggest that there are some aspects of that educative process that are specific to one group of individuals in exclusion of all others.

For example, those individuals with a hearing impairment need provision within an auditory domain that is a separate, compartmentalized issue for them (and therefore for their educators). They do need special treatment if they are to gain the same possibility of accessing curricula as their non-hearing-impaired peers. Indeed to deny them such special consideration for ideological reasons would be, in my view, to deny a necessary advantage in the search for inclusion. To indicate to an individual student with a hearing impairment that his or her needs for auditory support cannot be dealt with specifically (in this case by way of a separate chapter) because we have to include him or her in the whole of our approach to pedagogy 'first' is somewhat perverse. If the goal of inclusion is to be attained, it will only be by considering the specifics of need as well as a pedagogy for all. In short, to separate out a set of issues and give it special consideration is not to deny that the set is also embedded (included) in a greater whole – it is merely to suggest that to understand its place within the whole, one needs to understands the specifics that define it. And for those who find no definable specifics within hearing impairment or schizophrenia or dyslexia or similar conditions, I would suggest a careful reading of the case studies that underpin most of the chapters in this book.

The heterogeneity of learning needs

Certainly, it was the intention when I conceived of this book and its layout that contributing authors would consider the curriculum in such a way as to 'take account of the heterogeneity of learning needs'. Indeed what underpins the book is the notion that all students have different learning needs, and that each individual student comes to the learning context of a particular university with his or her own set of expectations, motivations, prior knowledge and experience, as well as levels of ability and skill across a range of intellectual and social domains that are specific to him or her alone. I would argue that in recognizing this heterogeneity, it is also possible to identify sets of learning characteristic within the continuum of differ-ence that can usefully be addressed in a direct and compartmentalized way. Indeed, as I have already noted, I would argue that to fail to address specific kinds of need in this direct way is to do a disservice to individuals who can only succeed when such attention is paid.

The university lecturer engages with large numbers of students every year. That lecturer may well recognize that those students are a heteroge-neous group, and try to devise and deliver a curriculum that meets all their needs. What this book seeks to do is to help that lecturer by giving direct information about the learning needs of particular groups of individuals, and advice on how best to adapt the curriculum and its delivery in such a way as to include individuals within those groups in an educative process that seeks to offer the best opportunities for successful learning for all.

The students' perspectives

The contributing authors in this book are all experienced in the area that they address in their respective chapters. Some have themselves disabilities, or difficulties with some aspects of learning. There is not however a specific chapter written by a disabled student giving her or his perspective on the experience of higher education. Rather the device has been used of incor-porating the student's view in each chapter by way of student comment and by case studies. Those views are taken to be of vital importance in the search for inclusion, and are built into the text in the various chapters. In this way it is hoped that the range of views and interpretations can be encompassed.

Rights and privileges

It is not the purpose of this book to consider in detail the specific legal situ-ation with regard to the rights and privileges of the disabled in higher education. Indeed the book considers a kind of teaching that is responsive to students who would not fall within the terms of the Disability Act: it contains a chapter on English as a second language. (Clearly the claim being made is not that this is a disability, but rather that it requires special teaching.) The book is intended to focus on issues of pedagogy that will hopefully transcend the particular period of time of publication and the immediate legal context. Nevertheless the various chapters are written within the current legal and social climate, and reflect a concern therefore with the issues that arise from recent legislation. In addition, the chapter by Jeremy Cooper (Chapter 2) does address issues within the legal scenario, taking an international perspective in order to set what is happening in the UK within a wider context. In this introductory chapter I touch upon some of the issues, but again from the point of view of pedagogy rather than of the specifics of legality or social change. I will however summarize the current situation with regard to disability very briefly in the section below.

Disability legislation – brief overview

The Disability Discrimination Act (DDA) gives those with disabilities a legal right to fair treatment in certain defined areas such as employment and the provision of services. Disability here is defined as 'mental or physical impairment that has a substantial and long term effect on the ability to carry out day to day activities' (again, I stress that this book transgresses this boundary). Basically this means that in the UK at present, those with disabilities must not be treated any less favourably than those without. Of course there are 'reasonable' limits to what is required of employers and to the kind of adjustments they are expected to make. In itself the DDA did not offer students protection from discriminatory practices in education, but universities were required to state to the funding council their present and future provision for disabled students. (This latter requirement has changed since later amendments to the Act.)

The Special Needs and Disability Act of 2001 amended the DDA and included education in Part IV. Effectively this amendment requires universities (among others) not to treat disabled students less favourably (without justification) than those who are not disabled, and to make reasonable adjustments to ensure that people who are disabled are not substantially disadvantaged in gaining access to the education on offer. The amendment is being staged in implementation at the time of writing this book, with the duty to make reasonable adjustments in terms of auxiliary aids and services coming into force in 2003, and to make physical adjustments by 2005. Guidance on the implementation of the Act is provided in a Statutory Code of Practice.

Curricular flexibility

It is incumbent upon higher educational institutions (HEIs) therefore to ensure that students with disabilities can participate fully in the curriculum, and that the kinds of educational activity contained within that curriculum have enough inbuilt flexibility to enable that participation. Again, in this book we are including in this aim students who have learning needs that require a special response from educators, but who do not fall within the definition of disabled. Such a process of enabling participation requires that HEIs analyse what they offer to their students and what expectations they have of them. This in itself is, of course, no bad thing. Working through what learning experiences are essential for a set of outcomes to be realized, and what 'performances' would legitimately count as indicators of a successful realization of those outcomes, is useful in the same way as any fundamental reappraisal of aims and ways of achieving and measuring them. In short, addressing the special needs of some learners is likely to lead to an enhancement of educators' understanding of their own implicit and explicit aims, and the processes by which they try to attain them. Seeing the procedures and outcomes of education from the perspective of the disabled may throw a new light on the process – elements of what have been established as custom and practice may be challenged by an examination of real purposes, to the benefit of all students.

In the current legislative climate in the UK, HEIs are required to review what courses require of students with declared disabilities, and where appropriate, reasonable adjustments must be made to those requirements so as to enable participation by such students. This makes sense where adjustments to learning processes, or the context within which those processes take place, can lead to the same opportunity for successful learning outcomes for all students. In my own view, the students whose needs are addressed in this book (whether or not they fall within the DDA) have the same right to the opportunity for successful learning as all other students.

Curricular additions and substitutes

If there is to be true inclusion within an HEI, then it is also clear that additional support needs to be provided by that HEI where it is necessary for all individuals to achieve desired learning outcomes. It may be that the extra support takes the shape of additional resources, or of additional courses that are embedded within the individual's overall programme of study. Clearly, what is needed here is for educators to think flexibly about ways of achieving the same goals but by different means. In this book it is the intention of contributors to challenge preconceived ways of designing and delivering the curriculum, and to offer ways in which educators can think outside traditional curricular parameters. This latter kind of thinking may involve creating educational activities that act as substitutes for those that are traditionally made available, and that are, for whatever reason, unavailable or inappropriate to the individual concerned. From a pedagogical point of view, the important thing about the substitute is, again, that it should act as an alternative means to the same (learning) end. From a legalistic point of view, words such as 'reasonable within the overall aims of the course' come into play. In Chapter 2, Jeremy Cooper draws attention to the way in which failure to provide the kinds of inclusive programme and their supplements indicated here may be seen as discriminatory.

Of the additional resources that are mentioned in the preceding paragraph, one common area of need is for course study materials to be made available in a non-traditional formats. It is important to note that, in terms of rights and privileges, the student who has special learning needs has not only a right to the conversion from traditional to non-traditional material (for example, printed text into Braille), but also the right not to be disadvantaged by the time taken for conversion. This notion of right of access without penalty runs as a theme throughout current legislation, but more importantly for our purpose here, is central to the creation of a pedagogy that includes all from the outset, and disadvantages none in the process of curriculum delivery. The notion pushes back the requirement to address differing needs to the stage where courses are conceived and accredited, or in the case of research students, to the point where individual programmes of study are negotiated.

Assessment

Similarly, students with disabilities have the right to a form of assessment that enables them to present their learning in a way that is not disadvantaged by any effects of that disability. Therefore, again, they have the right to conversion of assessment formats, and the right not to be disadvantaged in any way by that conversion. Educators need to conceive of the students discussed in this book as deserving of an equal opportunity to show what they can do and what they can learn. Adaptations of assessment processes may be required, to ensure this kind of equality of opportunity. It is also perhaps worth noting here that this applies to formative as well as summative assessment. Feedback on progress is important to any learner, and it may be that in terms of the special teaching that this book suggests is necessary, educators need to use initiative in finding ways of making feedback on all aspects of learning accessible and usable. Students need not only to be able to access feedback as a regular part of their engagement with the curriculum, but also be enabled to make the most effective use of that feedback.

Independent and critical thinking

The effective use of feedback noted above relates to the degree to which students can use the feedback they get – be it formal or informal – to inform their understanding of their own learning processes, and of the usefulness or otherwise of practical and intellectual strategies. Disabilities and difficulties of the kind discussed in this book should not require educators to narrow down their approach to pedagogy so that the delivery of knowledge and skills is seen to be of overriding importance, at the expense of developing individuals as independent and critical thinkers. I would argue that the whole of the educational process should be underpinned by the aim of enabling learners to become both independent and critical; certainly at the stage of higher education in particular, that aim should be realized, and all students should be included in that realization. In my own experience I have seen instances where lecturers, perhaps initially daunted by the educative task that faces them with particular individuals, have either consciously or unconsciously interpreted their teaching goals in untypically mechanistic and pragmatic terms. In short they have tended to 'teach to the test' rather than take a broader, more educative view. This is intended not as a criticism, but rather as a reflection on the hidden danger of focusing sharply on the difficulties raised by the individual's particular needs, and in so doing losing sight of the higher purposes of higher education. It is perhaps particularly important that this point is stressed here, at the outset of a book that does overtly focus on needs and ways of responding. As has been noted above, it is not the intention of contributing authors to deny the wider purposes of education, by attending to some of the necessary pragmatics of access and subsequent appropriate strategies for successful learning.

Guarding against the creation of new difficulties

Another issue of which educators perhaps need to remain aware as they plan for teaching in special situations is that of creating new problems when trying to resolve acknowledged difficulties. In Chapter 5, Archie Roy describes the difficulties that may be created for the visually impaired if specialist technological equipment is located – by dint of the very fact that it is special – separately from the technology used by other students engaging in the same work. In resolving the need of the visually impaired to have access to what is on the screen, it may be that a new isolation is created, and the opportunity for important interaction, both social and intellectual, between the visually impaired student and his/her peers is much diminished. A further right therefore is for all students to have their particular needs addressed without that address causing new difficulties or anomalies to arise.

Extra-curricular life

The experience of going to university is about more than attending lectures and seminars and engaging with assessments. The totality of the experience includes a strong element of the social, and involves the development of personality as well as intellect and skill. Those with the range of special learning needs discussed in this book have a right to enter into the extra-curricular life of the university according to their wishes, in the same way as those without such special needs. Therefore those within the HEI who have a responsibility for designing activities that fall outside the main academic curriculum need to conceive of that responsibility as including all students, regardless of disability. The same kind of adjustments and additions as within the academic curriculum may be necessary, and it is important to stress here that they are no less important. Again, specific chapters address particular issues in relation to particular kinds of disability and learning need.

Valuing diversity

A key principle that underpins this book is that the inclusion of students with disabilities and ways of learning that are outside the range commonly addressed in higher education is not simply a matter of striving to cope with new challenges. It is also a matter of valuing diversity. A truly inclusive society is one in which people are valued for themselves, and where the diverse aspects of their ways of living are valued as an enriching dynamic for that society. If readers can accept that universities are key players in the development of social mores, then clearly it is important that they recognize the principle, adhere to it and make apparent how valuing diversity enriches the processes of learning and achievement with which they are involved. By stressing 'making apparent' here, I am trying to indicate that universities can play an important role in changing stereotypical attitudes to people with disabilities. For example, there are a number of occasions in this book where examples are given of enrichment of the lives of all students in a learning group as a result of the inclusion of students with particular and special learning needs. I recognize that this is easy to write here, and may sound sentimental and even pious to the reader – but those who have enjoyed the experience of working and living with the students who are cited in this book may well testify to the power and long-lasting positive effect of that experience.

One aspect of that experience may be an appreciation of the ability and effort that has often gone into the achievement of reaching higher education and succeeding within it. Primarily of course, abilities and effort are within the individual student, but that is not to understate the contribution in these respects made by those around that student – both family and professional. Calling for a special kind of teaching is, in part at least, recognition of the efforts that will have predated the stage of higher education.

There is also a more pragmatic outcome to the kind of inclusion described in this book; it may well be that consideration of the curriculum, its delivery and assessment, brings about a clearer understanding of principles and purposes in the minds of educators, which in turn benefits all students. It may also be the case the provision of special resourcing for some ends up, directly or indirectly, benefiting all.

Individual differences

One of the dangers of setting out to try to give guidance about a range of students who will require special teaching is that, in categorizing by kind of disability, individual differences within conditions may be obscured. Contributing authors in this book are aware of this danger, and address the need to recognize individual differences within the area they discuss. Archie Roy points out, for example, that what is required for two students both diagnosed as 'partially sighted' will be very different where one has no central vision and the other no peripheral vision – large print will assist the former but not necessarily the latter.

It is also important to note that it is not just the range of differences of kind (such as difficulties in central as opposed to peripheral vision) within a condition that matters, but also the range of other aspects of the individual's learning characteristics, which make up the sum total of him/her as a learner. For example, in autism there is in the first place a continuum of 'autistic spectrum disorders' within which an individual may fall. But each individual also has a level of learning ability, a kind of learning style (albeit one that has been formed within the context of the disability), language ability, personality and so on, that is unique to him or her. It would be naïve to think that all individuals with autism are the same, and it would be educationally inappropriate to treat them as such. What is required of pedagogy is that the kinds of ways that individuals with autism approach problem-solving situations (taking problem solving here in its broadest sense) is taken as a template to interpret the way in which an individual student with autism is likely to set about tackling a specific set of learning tasks. From this interpretation, strategies can be devised that enable that individual to be as effective as possible in the learning situation.

The argument that underpins this book is that lecturers who intend to include all students in their teaching need to be aware, first, that the task of teaching involves operating on a set of templates in relation to the mechanics of teaching and learning (for example, that students will be motivated by the lecturer's enthusiasm for the subject – albeit to a greater or lesser extent), and second, that these templates may not apply to all (so those with autism are unlikely to be able to perceive at a fundamental level another person's enthusiasm, let alone make use of it). In short, teaching those who bring special learning characteristics to the teaching and learning scenario requires that lecturers consider their typical modes of operation, and reinterpret them in the light of the new evidence before them. The new evidence is in the form of understanding how different individuals gain access to the classroom in terms of its language (written or spoken), physical context, social interactions and so on. To repeat here a sentiment that is made elsewhere in this book, the claim is being made that this process of consideration and reinterpretation is enriching for all concerned. The effectiveness of the process of learning and teaching may be enhanced for all students and lecturers where the needs of some are given special consideration.

Special teaching

The use of the term 'special teaching' in the title of this book is intended to focus attention on the process of teaching that goes on in the higher education sector, and how that teaching needs to be conceived of as requiring flexibility and an openness to diversity. (This intention may be contrasted with one underpinned by an attitude that universities now need to focus on how to cope with students who enrol with special needs not previously encountered by many in the HE sector.) In my view what is required is a reconceptualization of teaching in HE, so that teaching includes from the outset and as a matter of course the capability and intent to take special measures for specific instances of learning needs. If there is to be a truly inclusive higher education system, then what counts as an effective pedagogy in universities must include special ways of addressing effectively all learning needs – whatever issues of curricular access and diverse learning style arise. This book aims to give readers understanding of specific examples of the diversity of learning needs, and indications of the kinds of skill and strategy that will enable them to meet those kinds of needs in their planning and delivery of the curriculum. It argues for a description of typical university teaching that includes the notion that special measures and special methods will be necessary, and therefore should be available to all educators. If effective learning for all is to be ensured, then those educators must be free, able and willing to apply those measures and methods appropriately.

Further reading

Cottrell, S M (2001) *Teaching Study Skills and Supporting Learning*, Palgrave, Basingstoke

Doyle, B (1996) *Disability Discrimination: The new law*, Jordans, London

Helios (1998) *European Guide of Good Practice: Towards equal opportunities for disabled people*, European Commission, Brussels

HMSO (1995) Disability Discrimination Act, HMSO, London

Hurst, A (1998) *Higher Education and Disability: An international perspective*, Ashgate Publishing, Aldershot

Hurst, A (1999) The Dearing Report and students with disabilities and learning difficulties, *Disability and Society*, **4**, (1) pp 65–83

Powers, S (1996) Inclusion is an attitude, not a place, Parts I and II, *Journal of the British Association of Teachers of the Deaf*, 20, pp 35–41 and 30, pp 65–69

Quality Assurance Agency for Higher Education (QAAHE) (1999) *Code of Practice for the Assurance of Academic Quality and Standards in Higher Education: Section 3, Students with Disabilities*, QAAHE, Gloucester

Scottish Higher Education Funding Council (SHEFC) (2000) *Teachability: Creating an accessible curriculum for students with disabilities*, SHEFC, Glasgow

Silver, P, Bourke, A and Strehorn, K (1988) Universal Instructional Design in HE: An approach for inclusion, *Equity and Excellence in Education*, 31, 47–51.

Wolfendale, S and Corbett, S (1996) *Opening Doors: Learning support in higher education*, Cassell, London

Part two

The context for change

2

From exclusion to inclusion: some lessons from abroad

Jeremy Cooper

Introduction

In the inclusive classroom, the student with a significant disability, regardless of the degree or nature of that disability, is a welcomed and valued member. The student is taught by the regular classroom teacher, who is supported as needed; follows the regular curriculum, with modification and adaptation; makes friends; and contributes to the learning of the entire class (Uditsky, 1993: 79). There are currently a number of significant changes taking place in the wider environment in the United Kingdom that should make it easier for students with disabilities to enter the inclusive classroom of higher education on a level playing field with their non-disabled peers, on terms approaching equality.

Since 2 October 2000, the European Convention on Human Rights has been incorporated directly into United Kingdom law, by virtue of the Human Rights Act 1998. This means that any 'public authority' (which includes higher education institutions) that breaches a Convention Right can be held directly accountable in the courts or tribunals of the United Kingdom. One of the key Convention Rights relates to education, and states that, 'No person shall be denied the right to education.'[1] There is a strengthening body of opinion that holds the belief that for a student with a disability, the only true meaning of the word 'education' is 'inclusive education'. For, as the Supreme Court of the United States eloquently stated in the groundbreaking decision of *Brown* v *Board of Education* in 1954, in the context of racially segregated education:

> In these days it is doubtful that any child may reasonably be expected to succeed in life if (s)he is denied the opportunity of an education. Such as opportunity ... must be made available on equal terms. ... To separate [students] from others of similar age and qualifications solely because of their [race] generates a feeling of inferiority as to their status in the community that may affect their hearts and minds in a way unlikely ever to be undone.
>
> (347 US 483, 1954)

Substitute the word disability for race, and the sentiments remain just as powerful.

Domestic law in the United Kingdom is starting to play an important role in strengthening the rights of disabled people to equal access to education. The Government has extended the range of the Disability Discrimination Act 1995 to include educational institutions (in the Special Educational Needs and Disability Rights Act 2000), and the Disability Rights Commission will be seeking to identify centres of excellence in which to develop best practice models. The Quality Assurance Agency, the government-funded central organization in the United Kingdom with responsibility for regulating standards of provision in all higher education institutions, has published a detailed Code of Practice setting out the standards that should be met to accommodate the needs of students with disabilities. The Code of Practice recognizes that disabled students are an integral part of the academic community, and states its belief that appropriate provision for students with disabilities is not additional or optional, but should be a core element in the overall educational provision of the institution (QAA, 2000).

In parallel with these developments in United Kingdom domestic law, the European Union is extending its non-discrimination directive to include the grounds of disability, which will cover employment and occupation, including conditions for access to employment and promotion, vocational guidance and training (Framework Directive for Equal Treatment in Employment and Occupation, 17 October 2000). The Directive must be fully enforced across the European Union by the year 2007.

Against this summary of developments in the United Kingdom, this chapter will take a wider view of access to higher education for disabled students, by looking for examples of the movement from exclusion to inclusion in three other major countries with strong liberal democracies,

Australia, Canada and the United States, to serve as useful benchmarks for ascertaining progress to date in the United Kingdom.

Australia

Approximately 7 per cent of the Australian population were said in 1990 to have a permanent physical disability (DEET, 1990). In Australia, the early 1990s showed a small, though statistically significant, increase in the numbers of the disabled population entering tertiary education institutions. This increase could be explained principally as the knock-on consequence of an improvement in schooling provision for students with disabilities in the 1980s (Leung, 1992: 7). In addition, in 1988 the Australian government formally recognized people with disabilities as a specific target group, requiring special programmes and assistance in preparation for study at tertiary level (Meekosha, Jackubowicz and Rice, 1991; Anderson, 1996). Developments in technological support were a subsequent factor increasing participation by people with disabilities in tertiary education (Anderson, 1996: 6; Murfitt, 1991; West *et al*, 1993). The second half of the decade saw a far faster growth in the numbers of students with disabilities entering tertiary education. Figures published in 2000 suggest that the number of students with disabilities such as deafness, vision impairment and dyslexia rose by 65 per cent between 1996 and 2000, with more than 18,000 such students now enrolled in tertiary education (Horin, 2000). The phenomenon of under-reporting, and the fact that some students have undiagnosed learning difficulties, means that this figure is probably even higher (Barr, Heavens and Parr, 1996).

Although as already indicated, this increase was in part a reflection of the more enlightened integrationist policies in secondary education that had been developing over the previous decade, the major catalyst for this expansion was the introduction in 1992 of the Federal Disability Discrimination Act, which included a section (Section 22) requiring academic institutions to be free from discrimination on the grounds of disability. The full text of the section reads as follows:

Section 22
(1) It is unlawful for an educational authority to discriminate against a person on the ground of the person's disability or a disability of any of the person's associates:
   (a) by refusing or failing to accept the person's application for admission as a student; or

      (b) in the terms or conditions on which it is prepared to admit the person as a student.

(2) It is unlawful for an educational authority to discriminate against a student on the ground of the student's disability or a disability of any of the student's associates:

      (a) by denying the student access, or limiting the student's access, to any benefit provided by the educational authority; or

      (b) by expelling the student; or

      (c) by subjecting the student to any other detriment.

(3) This section does not render it unlawful to discriminate against a person on the ground of the person's disability in respect of admission to an educational institution established wholly or primarily for students who have a particular disability where the person does not have that particular disability.

(4) This section does not render it unlawful to refuse or fail to accept a person's application for admission as a student at an educational institution where the person, if admitted as a student by the educational authority, would require services or facilities that are not required by students who do not have a disability and the provision of which would impose unjustifiable hardship on the educational authority.

The effect of this section is to make it unlawful for a tertiary institution to discriminate against people on the grounds of their disability. The institutions can free themselves from prima facie unlawful discrimination by making a reasonable adjustment to their policies, premises or practices wherever it is possible, necessary and reasonable to do so. 'The purpose of varying the usual policy or practice is to meet the needs of the person with a disability, rather than to accept practices developed with other circumstances in mind' (Jordan and Rodgers, 1999: 3). The principal constraint on this requirement is the defence of 'unjustifiable hardship'.

Section 22 (1) (a) has been considered at length in the two cases of *Finney* v *Hills Grammar School 1999* and *Hills Grammar School* v *HREOC 2000*. The cases determined the general procedures that should be followed by an educational institution when dealing with an application from a student with a disability. First, through a 'combined effort' involving both the applicant and the institution, agreement should be reached as to the range of services and facilities the applicant may require, by virtue of his or her disability. Second, the institution must consider what accommodation is required to meet these identified needs, drawing if necessary on expert opinion and advice. Third, the institution can make an assessment as to whether providing for these needs will impose an 'unjustifiable hardship' on it. It is only if an 'unjustifiable hardship' will be imposed upon it that an educational institution can refuse or fail to accept the enrolment of a student with a disability (Hannon, 2000: 35).

Cost is commonly used as an example of 'unjustifiable hardship' by educational institutions. One of the reasons the cost factor is especially significant in Australia is that the Federal Government provides no additional funding to cover the cost of providing extra services and facilities and services to meet a disabled student's needs (Horin, 2000). But the President of the Human Rights and Equal Opportunities Commission (HREOC), Sir Ronald Wilson, held in the 1995 case of *Scott* v *Telstra Corporation Ltd* that *all circumstances relevant to the benefit a person will gain* are to be taken into account and balanced against the cost in providing that benefit. 'These circumstances include social benefits such as increased independence, as well as economic opportunities' (Hannon, 2000: 36).

The term 'benefits' in the context of education has been considered at length by a number of bodies. The Adelaide Declaration[2] stated the benefits of education to include providing students with the qualities of self-confidence, optimism, high self-esteem and a commitment to personal excellence, as a basis for their potential life role as family, community and workforce members (Hannon, 2000: 40). And the Education 2000 Plan, issued by the NSW Department of School Education, describes educational benefits as including 'the development of skills and knowledge to enhance a student's quality of life and contributions to society, and the development of self confidence and esteem and respect for others' (Hannon, 2000: 40).

The Federal Department for Education, Training and Youth Affairs (DEYTA) issued in 2000 a set of Draft Disability Standards on Education. The standards cover the entire higher educational process, from enrolment through to exit. The standards are enacted under section 31 of the Disability Discrimination Act 1992, and unlike in the United Kingdom, standards issued in this way constitute a form of subordinate legislation. As such they have a formal status in law. An education authority, institution or provider must comply with the standards or it will be acting unlawfully. A breach of the standards will generate a right of complaint to the Human Rights and Equal Opportunities Commission under the relevant provisions of the Act.

The DEYTA has described the purpose of the standards in the following terms:[3]

Standards can help education providers comply with the Disability Discrimination Act, by clarifying their obligations and setting out how they can fulfil them. Equally, the standards can help students (and prospective students) with disabilities, or their associates, to understand their rights to education and training, and how these rights might be met. Providers must comply with these obligations to ensure they do not act unlawfully. The longer-term objective is to improve the education and training opportunities and outcomes for students and people with disabilities. Thus, the intention of standards is that students (and prospective students) with disabilities will be in a much better position to assess their rights under the Disability Discrimination Act, and education providers will likewise be given greater guidance on how to discharge their obligations under the Act.

The *obligations* set out in the standards are the legal standards with which education and training providers are obliged to comply. The *measures* accompanying each statement of obligation provide examples of actions that providers may take to ensure compliance with their legal obligations. In general, compliance with some or all of the measures will provide a defence against a complaint.

Under 'Enrolment,' the standards state that:

Prospective students with disabilities have the right to seek admission and enrol in an education or training institution, on the same basis and to the same extent as prospective students without disabilities. Prospective students with disabilities have the right to adjustments, which are necessary to ensure that they are able to be enrolled and complete enrolment processes without discrimination.

Education providers are obliged to ensure that prospective students with disabilities are not discriminated against in seeking admission and enrolment. Providers have an obligation to make reasonable adjustments, where necessary, to ensure that prospective students with disabilities are able to be considered for enrolment and complete enrolment processes without discrimination.

Measures to achieve this standard include ensuring that information about enrolment processes is inclusive and accessible to students with disabilities and their associates, and is available in a range of formats and within a reasonable time-frame. The range of formats may vary with the resources and purposes of the provider. All enrolment procedures should be designed so that students with disabilities, or their associates, can complete them without undue hardship. Information about the choice of programmes and courses of study, progression and settings must be accessible and sufficient for students with disabilities, or their associates, to make informed decisions.

The standards require that, once enrolled, students with disabilities should enjoy the same *rights and privileges* as students without disabilities:

Education providers are obliged to ensure that students with disabilities are not discriminated against in participating in the programmes and services, and using the facilities, provided by the education or training institution. Providers are obliged to negotiate with the students with disabilities, or their associates, and implement any reasonable adjustments necessary to ensure that students with disabilities are afforded substantive equality in participating in educational programmes and services.

Measures to enable such full participation might include ensuring that educational activities are sufficiently flexible to enable students with disabilities to undertake them. Course requirements should be reviewed, in the light of information provided by students with disabilities or their associates, to include activities to enable participation by students with disabilities, and necessary adjustments made in the light of this information. Additional support, such as bridging or enabling courses, should be provided as part of the educational programme of students with disabilities, where necessary, to assist them achieve the intended learning outcomes. Where a course necessarily includes an activity in which a student with a disability cannot participate, the student should be offered an activity that constitutes a reasonable substitute within the context of the overall aims of the course. Activities conducted in non-classroom settings, or extra-curricular activities, or activities that are part of the broader educational programme, should be designed to include students with disabilities.

On the question of curriculum development, course accreditation and delivery:

Students with disabilities have the same rights as other students to participate in educational programmes or courses that develop their skills, knowledge and understanding, including relevant supplementary programmes.

Education providers are [subject to maintaining the academic requirements of the course] obliged to ensure that students with disabilities are not discriminated against in participating in educational programmes or courses that develop their skills, knowledge and understanding, including relevant supplementary programmes. Providers have an obligation to make reasonable adjustments necessary to ensure that students with disabilities are afforded substantive equality in opportunities to participate in learning experiences and complete assessment and certification requirements.

Measures to achieve the above goals might include ensuring curriculum, course and teaching materials, assessment and certification are appropriate, inclusive and accessible. Course delivery modes and learning activities should take account of the intended educational outcomes and the learning capacities and needs of students with disabilities. Course study materials should be made available in appropriate formats, and where conversion of materials into alternative accessible formats is required, students should not be disadvantaged by the time taken for conversion. Teaching and delivery strategies should be adjusted to meet the learning needs of students with disabilities, and address any disadvantage in their learning resulting from their disabilities, including provision of additional support, such as bridging or enabling courses. Assessment procedures and methodologies should be adapted to enable students with disabilities to demonstrate the knowledge, skills or competencies being assessed.

On student support services:

Students with disabilities, like other students, have the right to use student support services provided by education authorities and institutions, in addition to the right to any specialized services provided by education authorities and institutions and other agencies in the health and community services sector. These services include specialist expertise and/or support for personal and medical care, without which some students with disabilities would not be able to access education and training.

Education authorities and institutions have an obligation not to discriminate against students with disabilities in relation to support services used by students in general. Education authorities and institutions have an obligation to provide special support services that enable students with disabilities to participate in education. The authority or institution may provide these services alone or in collaboration with the health and community services sectors. They are also obliged to make any reasonable adjustments necessary to ensure access for students with disabilities to support services used by students in general.

Measures to enable the exercise of these rights include the making of adjustments to enable students with disabilities to access services provided for students in general, and collaborative arrangements with specialized service providers including health, personal care, and therapies such as speech, occupational and physiotherapy. The provision of specialized equipment to support students with disabilities in participating in education and training, including adaptive technology, assistive devices and equipment, including applications of emerging technologies, is another possible measure. And the making available of appropriately trained support staff to assist students with disabilities, such as specialist teachers, interpreters, note-takers and teacher's aides, provides a further example.

The standards contain a set of detailed provisions designed to prevent harassment and victimization, and set out circumstances in which 'special measures' can be authorized to take affirmative action to the benefit of students with disabilities, for example programmes or initiatives that afford students with disabilities, or with a particular disability, benefits, grants, goods, or access to facilities, services or opportunities to meet their special needs.

Most Australian universities now have a written Disability Action Plan, which they have lodged with the HREOC, whose task it is to advise on and monitor its development and realization. Some of these plans are extremely detailed. For example, the section of the Plan of the Griffith University on Alternative Assessment for Students with Disabilities alone runs to 26 pages, and the Australian National University policy on oral examinations for students with disabilities is equally impressive (Jordan, 1992). Significantly, the policies are underpinned by persuasive research demonstrating that reading scores of students with a learning disability were not significantly different when both groups were allowed extra time (Runyan, 1991). Similarly, evidence is adduced that a test's construct and predictive validities were unlikely to be jeopardized by time variations (Lin, 1986). It seems that in Australia the universities are, by and large, 'walking the talk', and thereby instil confidence in the academic community, that differential assessment is not a threat to academic standards.

Canada

Canada was the first country in the world to include a full and unequivocal equality clause in the wording of its constitution. The Canadian Charter of Rights and Freedoms, Paragraph 15 (1) states as follows:

> Every individual is equal before and under the law and has the right to the equal protection and equal benefit of the law without discrimination based on race, national or ethnic origin, colour, religion, sex, age, *or mental or physical disability.*

The use of the phrase 'equal protection and equal benefit' is especially striking. It enables a debate on the 'benefits of education' akin to the

Australian debates outlined above, to be cast in a constitutional legal framework. In Canada, discrimination in the provision of education, and of its benefits, can be directly challenged in the courts.

All Canadian universities have special units advising and supporting disabled students.[4] A typical policy statement is that to be found in the University of New Brunswick as follows:

> The University of New Brunswick is committed to equitable treatment of students with disabilities. While all students are expected to satisfy the requirements for courses and programs, the administration, faculty, staff, and students of UNB are expected to provide reasonable accommodation to meet the needs of students with disabilities. Reasonable accommodation is the use of originality and flexibility in adjusting to particular needs; it is not to be interpreted as the lowering of standards. Reasonable accommodations may include such things as special seating, wheelchair accessible tables, adjustments to lighting and ventilation, use of a computer, tape recorder or FM system, and expanded time for tests or exams. This statement recognizes the responsibility of the student to identify his/her specific needs for which accommodation is requested; it also recognizes the role of the university to preserve, as much as possible, the confidentiality and privacy of students' affairs; and finally it recognizes the joint effort of student and university needed to create and support an environment where students with disabilities will have the opportunity to attain academic and personal success.

The pattern is thus very close to that found in the Australian examples, discussed above. But as in Australia, it is also constrained by the reasonable allocation of resources:

> UNB has limited resources and must work within existing resources (faculty, staff and budgets) in attempting to meet the needs of students with disabilities.

Another impressive example of a dynamic approach to seeking equality for students with disabilities is provided by the University of Manitoba, whose Disability Services Unit is 'organized to promote a learning environment which is accessible to students with disabilities, by coordinating services and programs for these students, providing information regarding the educational implications of disabilities, and enhancing awareness of disability issues.'

The services for students with disabilities, including students with temporary disabilities (breaks, sprains, or other injuries), include registrations assistance, on-campus transportation, elevator and lift keys access, test and exam accommodations (such as taped questions, enlarged print, wheel-chair accessible space), specialized equipment access for exams and tests (such as VTEKS, four-track tape recorders, voice synthesis, 19 inch moni-tors, word processors, and Perkins Brailer), volunteer readers and note takers, and audio-taped texts from the Special Materials Branch of the Manitoba Department of Education.

The University of Saskatchewan has a 37 page, fully comprehensive University Policy for Students with Disabilities, with a preamble that encapsulates the concepts of equal protection and benefits, but also adds the important further dimension of valuing diversity, a key positive concept in the process of changing stereotypical attitudes towards people with disabil-ities:

> Just as we value the diversity of all our students, we value and appreciate the differences and perspectives that students with disabilities bring to Campus. We appreciate the efforts, the determination and the compensatory strategies that they have developed to enable them to enrol in University. We value what we learn about disabilities; this enriches us individually and it enriches the learning environment.

In Canada, claims of discrimination on the grounds of disability are referred in the first instance to the Canadian Human Rights Commission. Standing alongside the Commission is the Canadian Human Rights Tribunal, an independent body responsible for adjudicating complaints referred to it by the Canadian Human Rights Commission. The Commission refers a complaint to the Tribunal when it believes an inquiry is warranted.

United States

The United States is a third jurisdiction in which legislation recognizing the rights of students (both actual and potential) to be protected against discrimination is well entrenched in both the statute books and the culture of the nation. Three sets of laws deal specifically with disability discrimina-tion in the context of education. The first is the Individuals with Disabilities Education Act 1975 (IDEA).[5] Although the Act does not apply to third-tier education (further or higher education), it has nevertheless been an impor-tant tool in assisting disabled youngsters to progress through mainstream school education in the least restrictive environment possible, thereby strengthening their chances of entering higher education on equal terms. This has been achieved by such entitlements as the interactive development of an Individualized Education Programme (IEP) for each disabled pupil, setting out the attainments, goals, examining methods and resources he or she will receive, together with 'related services'. IEP is designed to help children with disabilities take maximum advantage of the educational opportunities offered to others, without discrimination. At the heart of this legislation is a statutory presumption that all children are entitled to main-stream, unsegregated education. In 1997, the legislation was further enhanced to enable greater parent participation in the process, to widen the agenda of the IEP, and to improve school administration (Annino 1999; Quinn, 1999: 7).

The second set of protections is contained in the Rehabilitation Act 1973, which states:

> No *otherwise qualified* handicapped individual shall, solely by reason of his handicap, be excluded from participation in, be denied the benefits of, or be subjected to discrimination under any program or activity receiving federal financial assistance.
> (s. 504)

The Act covers both direct and indirect discrimination, and also includes the requirement of reasonable accommodation, to counter the potential discriminatory impact of a barrier or an excluding practice. The Act is however limited to the Federal sector of government, and to 'those private entities that are in sufficiently close financial proximity to that sector' (Quinn, 1999: 8). But the majority of universities in the United States rely upon some form of Federal funding, and are therefore subject to the provisions and the sanctions of this section.

The third, and most important, piece of legislation to have been introduced in the United States in this field was the Americans with Disabilities Act 1990 (ADA). Although unlike the Canadian and Australian models considered earlier, the ADA makes no specific reference to discrimination in the field of education, its anti-discriminatory remit extends to the provision of all public services, and thus includes all public universities and colleges, and to the provision of private goods and services when they constitute 'public accommodations', which includes most of the other activities of private universities and colleges. When linked together with the Rehabilitation Act, the protection afforded is fairly comprehensive. It is significant to note that the percentage of college entrants reporting disabilities rose from 2.6 per cent in 1978 to 8.8 per cent in 1991 to 9.2 per cent in 1994, an increase which coincides very clearly with the impact of the new legal rights (Thompson, 1997: 1A). Disability rights-based litigation in higher education has also been on the increase, reflecting the key proactive role played by the courts in furthering the parameters of rights (Rothstein, 1994).

Under the combined legislation, people are deemed to be disabled if they have a 'physical or mental impairment that substantially limits one or more major life activity, or a history of such an impairment, or are regarded by others as having such an impairment.' They can claim discrimination if:

1. By reason of their disability, they have been excluded from participation in, or denied the benefits of the programme of study and related activities.

and

2. They are 'otherwise qualified' to meet and perform the essential components of the programme of study and related activities, if necessary as a result of a 'reasonable adjustment' by the institution in question, to allow such participation. A failure to make 'reasonable adjustments' in policies, practices and procedures to accommodate the person's disability is deemed explicitly to be a 'discriminatory act' under the ADA. (ADA s. 302 (20 (A) (ii).)

So what has been the practical effect of all this legislation upon the ability of people with disabilities to access and benefit from higher education provision in the United States? Gerard Quinn, Director of the Disability Law and Policy Research Unit in the University of Galway, Ireland has carried out a detailed analysis of the litigation initiated by students with disabilities in the United States under the above legislation (Quinn, 1999). (See also Edwards, 1997; Rothstein 1997.) According to Quinn, most cases have involved students with disabilities expelled from their college programmes, who subsequently sued the authorities for failing to provide reasonable accommodation in response to their disability. He found that the majority of the cases were unsuccessful. He cites two reasons for this (Quinn, 1999: 10). First, many students were unable to convince the courts that they were in fact 'otherwise qualified' to pursue the course of studies in the relevant programme. Second, the courts were frequently unwilling to accept that the particular form of accommodation requested by the student was 'reasonable', as its introduction would fundamentally alter the nature of the programme in question.

Several cases illustrate the first point. The common theme is that accommodations cannot be allowed to reduce the minimum academic baseline standards of the institution, under a cloak of anti-discrimination policy. For example, in *Robinson* v *Hamline University 1994*,[6] a law student was admitted to law school under its affirmative action programme, and was subsequently discovered to have mild reading and writing learning disabilities. Despite being given a reduced workload, extra time in examinations, and many individual tutoring sessions, he failed to reach the minimum level required to progress, and was subsequently expelled from the school, which was the normal procedure in these circumstances. He claimed disability discrimination, alleging a failure on the part of the institution to provide him with reasonable accommodation. His claim was rejected on the grounds, inter alia, that '[further accommodations] would have given Robinson an unfair advantage and would have caused other students to believe they were being treated unfairly.'[7] In *McGregor* v *Louisana State University Board of Supervisors*,[8] a law student was deemed not qualified to progress, having repeatedly failed to meet minimum grade requirements, notwithstanding numerous and extensive reasonable adjustments by the institution. The Appeals Court rejected the student's subsequent appeal, applying the same reasoning as in the Robinson case, namely that 'the additional accommodations sought (in-home examinations) would constitute preferential treatment and go beyond eliminating disadvantageous treatment'.[9]

A further set of cases illustrate the second point. In *Ohio Civil Rights Commission* v *Case Western Reserve University 1994*, a blind student applied to attend medical school, which was a prerequisite to achieving her ultimate goal, to become a qualified psychiatrist. It was accepted that she would be unable to carry out such activities as taking blood, or putting up an intravenous drip, but she argued that none of these activities was essential to becoming a psychiatrist. Rejecting her appeal against the Medical School's refusal to admit her, the Appeal Court held that 'the accommodations required to graduate her from [the Medical School] would leave her with far less than the full medical experience required by [Medical School] graduates'. The Ohio Supreme Court upheld this position, arguing that the requested accommodations would fundamentally alter the nature of the programme.[10]

In *Maczacyj* v *New York*,[11] a graduate arts student suffered from panic attacks, had great difficulty in classroom situations, and had requested access to the classroom via a satellite link-up. The request was refused by the college, and challenged by the student as discriminatory. But the college's refusal was upheld by the Federal District Court, on the grounds that class attendance was an essential element of the programme, which involved the assessment of student presentations and other forms of interaction. In

Wynne v *Tufts University School of Medicine*,[12] the Federal Appeal Court upheld the decision of the Medical School to refuse to give a student with cognitive difficulties an alternative test to the usual multiple choice format, on the grounds that accommodating the student in this way would unduly affect the programme of study by lowering its academic standards.

One issue that is being followed especially closely at present in the United States is the legality of the practice of flagging non-standard test scores in admissions to institutions of higher education. Under this practice, students with disabilities that allow them special accommodations in the entrance admission assessment process (for example, extra writing time, separate accommodation, a reader or a scribe) find that their examination scripts are then 'flagged' to indicate to the examiner that they were given a special accommodation. In the words of one commentator, 'Although the label does not say DISABILITY in bold letters, university admissions departments undoubtedly know what it means. This policy invites discrimination by those educational institutions that would prefer not to have people with disabilities on their campus.'[13] Extensive analysis of the issue by Mayer (1998: 521) has concluded that the practice constitutes a discriminatory practice under both the Rehabilitation Act and the ADA, and advocates that the practice be therefore abandoned. (See also Quinn, 2001.)

Conclusion

This brief analysis of developments in the rights of students with disabilities to demand full inclusion in the higher educational experience of their peers without disabilities provides a clear message to the United Kingdom. The road to progress lies in the development of proactive coalitions between legislators prepared to introduce comprehensive anti-discrimination laws, and higher education authorities and quality monitoring bodies (including disability rights activists and lawyers) who have the capacity and will to enforce these laws via comprehensive and enforceable Codes of Practice.

References

Anderson, J (1996) *Issues and Barriers in Postgraduate Education for People who Have a Disability*, Report for the DEET Co-operative Project, Victoria, Australia

Annino, P (1999) The 1997 Amendments to the IDEA: improving the quality of special education for children with disabilities, *Mental Health and Physical Disability Law Reporter*, 23, Jan/Feb, p 125

Barr, R, Heavens, K and Parr, P (1996) *The Needs and Experiences of Tertiary Students with a Learning Disability*. Conference Proceedings, Pathways III Conference, University of Western Sydney, Australia

Department of Employment, Education and Training (DEET) (1990) *A Fair Chance for All*, DEET, Canberra, Australia

Edwards, R (1997) The rights of students with learning disabilities and the responsibilities of institutions of higher education under the ADA, *Journal of Law and Policy*, 2, pp 213–37

Framework Directive (2000) Framework Directive for Equal Treatment in Employment and Occupation, 17 October 2000. 12490/00, European Commission

Hannon, M (2000) The Disability Discrimination Act 1992: protection against discrimination in the provision of education, in *Explorations on Law and Disability in Australia*, ed M Jones and L Basser Marks, pp 28–53, Federation Press, Annandale, Australia

Horin, A (2000) Disabled students 'neglected,' *Sydney Morning Herald*, 28 October

Jordan, M (1992) *Managing Oral Examinations for Students with Disabilities: A Guide for Staff and Students*, Australian National University, Canberra, Australia

Jordan, M and Rodgers, N (1999) *Alternative Assessment for Students with Disabilities*, Griffith University Academic Administration, Brisbane, Australia

Leung, P (1992) Keynote address, *Australian Disability Review*, 2 , pp 3–13

Lin, M (1986) *The Impact of Time Limits on Test Behaviours*, Paper presented at the Annual meeting of the American Educational Research Association, San Francisco

Mayer, K (1998) Flagging nonstandard test scores in admissions to institutions of higher education, *Stanford Law Review*, **50**, pp 469–522

Meekosha, H, Jackubowicz, A and Rice, E (1991) *Ethnic Minorities and Equity Strategies in Tertiary Education*, Centre for Multicultural Studies, University of Wollongong, New South Wales, Australia

Murfitt, K (1991) *Feasibility Study for the Establishment of a 24-Hour House Attendant Care Service at a Victorian University Campus*, Deakin University, Victoria, Australia

Quality Assurance Agency (QAA) (2000) *Code of Practice for the Assurance of Academic Quality and Standards in Higher Education*, Quality Assurance Agency for Higher Education, Gloucester

Quinn, G (1999) *Maintaining Academic Excellence and Achieving Equal Opportunities: An assessment of litigation involving students against American universities*, paper presented at the AHEAD Conference on Dyslexia and Third Level Education, Trinity College, Dublin

Quinn, G (2001) *The Flagging of Non-Standard Test Scores: A practice under legal retreat and in retreat in the United States*, Disability Law and Policy Research Unit, NUI, Galway

Rothstein, L (1994) College students with disabilities: litigation trends, *Review of Litigation*, **13**, p 425

Rothstein, L (1997) Higher education law symposium: higher education and disabilities: trends and developments, *Stetson Law Review*, **27**, pp 119–97

Runyan, M (1991) The effect of extra time on reading comprehension scores for university students with and without learning difficulties, *Journal of Learning Disabilities*, **24** (2), pp 104–8

Thompson, C (1997) More disabled students join college ranks, *St Louis Post*, 19 May

Uditsky, B (1993) From integration to inclusion: the Canadian experience, in *Is There a Desk with My Name On It? The politics of integration*, ed R Slee, Falmer Press, London

West, M, Kregal, J, Getzel, E, Zhu, M, Ipsen, S and Martin, E (1993) Beyond sector satisfaction and empowerment of students with disabilities in higher education, *Exceptional Children*, **59** (5), pp 456–67

Notes

1. First Protocol, Article 2, Human Rights Act 1998 Schedule One. The sub-clause to Article 2 further states that 'in the exercise of any functions which it assumes in relation to education and to teaching, the State shall respect the right of parents to ensure such education and teaching in conformity with their own religious and philosophical convictions'.

2. In April 1999, State, Territory and Commonwealth Ministers of Education met as the Ministerial Council on Education, Employment, Training and Youth Affairs (MCEETYA) in Adelaide. At that meeting, Ministers endorsed a new set of National Goals for Schooling in the Twenty-First Century. The new goals were released in April 1999 as *The Adelaide Declaration (1999) on National Goals for Schooling in the Twenty-First Century.*

3. Full text obtainable from http://www.detya.gov.au

4. For full details go to Web site http://ww2.mcgill.ca/StuServ/osd/unvir.htm

5. Originally enacted in 1975 as the Education of all Handicapped Children Act, but renamed in 1990 to emphasize that rights come before disabilities.

6.   Minn. Ct. App May 10, 1994.
7.   Ibid, cited in 18 *Mental and Physical Disability Law Reporter*, July/Aug 1994, 428.
8.   E.D. La, July 24, 1992.
9.   Ibid, cited in 18 *Mental and Physical Disability Law Reporter*, Jan/Feb 1994, 94–5.
10.   It is worth noting however that two of the Supreme Court judges put in a strong dissenting opinion, concluding that 'this is a case of prejudice, pure and simple'. Cited in 20 *Mental and Physical Disability Law Reporter*, July/Aug 1996, 551.
11.   956 F. Supp 403 WDNY (1997).
12.   926 F. 2d (1992).
13.   Letter on file at Stanford University, cited in Mayer (1998: 469).

3

Communications and information technology (C&IT) for disabled students

Martyn Cooper[1]

Introduction

The C&IT context in higher education

All students at higher education level now use computers in their learning. Increasingly, significant elements of courses are mediated by computer. Lecture notes, seminar topics, reading lists and so on are posted on course Web sites. The computer is used not only for reporting work, as a tool in research, and for data analysis, but also in labs to control experiments. There is increasing use of multimedia learning activities (such as virtual science approaches). Computers are used to support communications between students and between the students and their tutors by e-mail, discussion lists and online forums. For disabled people to be able to study at higher education level, they must be enabled to use a computer and participate fully in the computer-based activities of both their courses and the wider university context.

Many countries are developing legislation making it illegal to discriminate against disabled people in education (see Chapter 2). In the UK the key legislation is the Special Educational Needs and Disability Act 2001 (SENDA).[2] This legislates that education providers must not treat a disabled person less favourably for any reason that relates to the person's disability.

Further, the education provider is required to make reasonable adjustments to enable a disabled person to participate in its courses. Access to the IT facilities and computer-related elements of its courses is an important area where, by considering the needs of disabled students, discrimination can be prevented. Further it is where, if necessary, reasonable adjustments can readily be made to meet the needs of individual students with disabilities.

Objectives for this chapter

In response to the imperative that higher education students with disabilities need to be fully enabled to use a computer, this chapter sets out to:

1. Give an overview of how different disabilities may impinge on the student's use of a computer, and what tools are available to facilitate disabled students' access to IT.
2. Give pointers to what responses (reasonable adjustments) a higher education institution (HEI) and its individual lecturing/support staff need to make, to ensure that the computer-mediated sections of the curriculum are accessible to disabled students.
3. Indicate some additional resources, sources of information and services that may assist in ensuring that an HEI and individual members of its staff carry out their responsibilities in meeting the IT-related needs of both their current and anticipated disabled students.

Scope

This chapter focuses on the use of computers, and does not cover other technological support that it may be necessary to make available to disabled students: for example, loop systems for hearing aid users in lecture theatres. Nor does it consider where human support, such as note takers or sign language interpreters, may be more appropriate (these issues are dealt with elsewhere in this volume – notably in the case of the examples given here, in Chapter 4). In this chapter the terms C&IT and IT are used interchangeably.

Communications, information technology and the disabled learner

For disabled students to fully access the curriculum, they need access to a computer. Now virtually all disabled people can be enabled to make effective use of a computer. This section outlines the different means that can be employed to do this. The following section (Making the curriculum accessible) outlines the principles that must be applied in developing educational software or Web-based content to ensure that it is accessible to disabled students.

Enabling effective use of a computer

Some disabled students use accessibility features provided by the operating systems of the computer, and/or specialist software or hardware, to facilitate their use of the computer. These software or hardware tools are often referred to collectively as 'assistive technology'. If it is to be accessible to disabled students, any software or content mediated by the computer has to be developed so that it is compatible with these tools. This section provides an overview of the range of assistive technology available and the types of student it may benefit. It is, however, beyond the scope of this book to provide detailed guidelines on supporting an individual student by selecting the most appropriate assistive technology to meet his or her needs.

It is generally unhelpful to consider medical classifications of disability when seeking to identify the means of enabling people with disabilities to make efficient use of the computer. It is preferable to consider the abilities and disabilities of the individual, with respect to what they need to do to make most effective use of the computer; in other words, to take a functional approach. The functions to be considered fall into two broad categories:

1. How the person may best input commands and information into the computer (here most computer users use the keyboard and mouse).
2. How the person receives the output from the computer (for most computer users this will generally be the monitor, but also includes loudspeakers and printers).

The way in which these functions can be supported by mainstream and specialist tools is described in the following sections.

Computer input methods

Many disabled people will choose to use a conventional keyboard, since these generally present no problem to, for example, people with a visual impairment. They normally readily learn to touch-type. A simple key-guard (a rigid sheet with finger holes for each key laid over a conventional keyboard), can help those with a tremor or weak hands or arms, preventing them from hitting keys in error. However, for those who find a conventional QWERTY keyboard difficult or impossible to use, there are a great many alternatives available. Some of the available alternatives are listed here:

- Alternative keyboard configurations: these include larger and smaller sized versions, and keyboards configured for single-handed use or to reduce repetitive strain.
- Virtual keyboards for switch users. Some disabled people with severe physical disabilities elect to use a single switch, or combination of a small number of switches, which they operate with any body movement over which they have consistent control. To enable them to type, switches can be used as inputs to a variety of virtual keyboards. These virtual keyboards are software applications that run on the computer being controlled. They usually display a layout of letters and numbers on the computer monitor, and offer a range of scanning and word prediction features to facilitate efficient typing. Some communication aids that non-speakers use, often similarly controlled by switches, can act as direct replacements for computer keyboards.
- Speech recognition: since the mid-1990s, speech recognition software has become readily available. Here the words spoken by the user are translated into typed input into any application on the computer, or the commands to control the application. With practice, efficient input can be achieved through speech recognition. In many speech recognition programmes it is necessary for the user to announce each word individually; however, continued development is improving the situation here, so that the user can speak more naturally. Users must correct mistranslations, which will probably occur more frequently than typos for an average keyboard user. However the computer's accuracy of recognition improves with use.
- Alternatives to the mouse: there is a wide variety of pointing devices that can be used instead of the mouse. These include joysticks and trackballs than can offer different benefits. Some can, for instance, be operated by foot, while others minimize the effect of tremor on cursor movement. For those who cannot or choose not to use any of these, effective control can be enabled via the keyboard alone. The action of a mouse can be emulated by use of the arrow keys, but it is normally preferable to use keyboard shortcuts that achieve the same functionality as pointing and clicking a mouse at a menu, button on the display or a 'hot spot'.

Notes on the implications of alternative keyboards

A consideration when working through the implications of using different keyboard alternatives is the distinction between direct and indirect alternatives. A direct alternative to the conventional keyboard is one that connects to the computer via the keyboard port: for example single-handed, Braille or chord keyboards. An indirect alternative to a conventional keyboard does not use the keyboard port: for example onscreen virtual keyboard, voice recognition software, or touch-screen software.

Because indirect alternatives depend on software running on the computer being used by the students, there can be issues of compatibility between this software and the programmes that the students need to use. A direct alternative does not in general give rise to any such problems. However indirect alternatives may offer features that are important to improve the speed of entry for the user, such as scanning strategies or word prediction.

Some students with disabilities are only able to 'type' at speeds significantly slower than would be expected of most students. This has implications for how these students are best supported in their studies, and can have particular implications for examinations. Such students will generally require more time to give a fair account of themselves. This issue is covered further under 'Educational assessment' below.

Computer output

Screen-readers and Braille displays

In order to access computer output, individuals with no useful sight use software known as a 'screen-reader', which presents the textual content of the screen to either a speech synthesizer or a Braille display. A speech synthesizer can be either a hardware or software component, and can produce a range of synthetic voices. A Braille display consists of an array of plastic 'pins' that move up and down to create dynamically the dot pattern of a line of Braille. Users read the Braille by passing their finger(s) over the characters as the line of text is 'scanned'. Braille displays are used by fewer people than speech synthesizers. Less than 20 per cent of blind people are fluent Braille readers, although this percentage may be higher among blind students. Another factor that deters the use of Braille displays is their high cost.

Screen-readers enable the user to navigate the screen in a systematic way in order to read the contents of windows, dialogue boxes, menus and so on. Blind people are usually unable to use a mouse or similar pointing device, because they cannot see the position of the cursor on the screen. To enable blind people to access software, it is essential that all functions are available to screen-reading software, and can be accessed from keyboard commands, and for all graphical elements to have meaningful text labels. Additional approaches exist that can provide those without sight access to graphical material including tactile diagrams[3] and haptic displays (that rely on the sense of touch). Dedicated design is required for the former, and the use of the latter by blind students is still largely the object of research rather than common practice.

Screen magnification and display formatting

Partially sighted people have differing needs in terms of accessing a computer. Some require high levels of magnification, which can be provided by screen magnification software. This software can magnify the whole screen, or act as an on-screen magnifying glass, magnifying only the area surrounding the cursor, and can also provide different levels of magnification. Some screen magnifiers can be used in conjunction with a speech synthesizer, which provides speech output as an additional support.

As well as magnification, partially sighted people may benefit from other adaptations to the way in which information is presented. High contrast between text and the background, and different colour combinations, can make text more readable for some. Screen magnifying software and the ability to select preferred character sizes and contrasting colour schemes are provided as standard on Windows and Mac computers. Users can select the viewing conditions that best suit them, which will then be applied to most programmes running on that computer without the need for separate adjustments in each programme. Screen magnifiers are also available separately as software packages.

A large screen (over 53 cm (21 in)) can also be of benefit to those with partial sight. For input to the computer, most partially sighted people can use a mouse; large print keyboard labels exist to render the keyboard more visible for those who are unable to touch-type.

Auditory outputs and hearing impairment

In general, people who are deaf or have impaired hearing do not require any specific assistive technology in order to use a computer effectively. People who have some useful hearing may require control over the volume and tone of audio outputs, or coupling to their hearing aids. However if an educational software application makes extensive use of sound, alternatives need to be provided for deaf/hearing impaired users. This will normally consist of a transcript of the recorded speech. In such cases the software developer needs to consider how a deaf person would navigate to and access the text alternatives.

Deaf-blindness

People who are deaf-blind can access computers using a standard keyboard for input and a Braille display to access the output in the same way as some blind people.

Dyslexia (specific learning disabilities)

Students with dyslexia may use a wide range of display modifications and assistive technologies. In general, such students have difficulty reading on-screen text, and may also have difficulty in composing and physically typing their own work. This group can be supported by assistive technology for both input and output. For those who have difficulty with inputting into the computer, voice recognition can be useful to compose written work. Those who have difficulty reading on-screen text can use software to change the presentation of the text. The type of presentation depends on the specific needs of the individual, but many find it useful to change the size, character spacing, line spacing, and line length of text on the screen. In addition, different combinations of text and background colour can make text more readable. People who have difficulty reading may also find it useful to have text read aloud by text-to-speech software. Readers may wish to refer here to Chapter 8.

Software configuration/adaptations

Over the last 10 years or so, operating systems have increasingly incorporated features that enable disabled people to use the computer more readily. (On a Windows PC, see the optional features under Start/Programmes/Accessories/Accessibility.) Typical examples here include 'sticky keys' which enable features to be accessed by pressing keys sequentially that would normally require more than one key to be depressed simultaneously (eg Ctrl/Alt/Del). Basic screen magnification is also usually provided. Disabled students may need support in selecting which of these tools are helpful to them, and configuring them on their computer and to work with their software applications.

Another facility that has become increasingly important is the use of personal style sheets. These define, for example, in what size and colours text and background should be displayed when viewing a Web page in a browser. For these to be used, the content provider needs to configure its pages so that the users' own style sheets can override the default presentation style.

In a campus situation, where a student may be using a variety of university-provided computers at different times, there is much to be gained by implementing individual user profiles, with configuration files being accessed by any machine at log-in. This greatly reduces the effort required in providing effective IT support to large user numbers. Where this is done, the provision should also include in the profile any accessibility features or assisitive technology the particular student uses. Since most network technologies and operating systems now provide for such features, this is often more a policy issue than a technical one.

Issues with some software packages when using assistive technologies

Problems can occur when students need to use a particular software package for their course and this proves to be incompatible with the assistive technology they use. This incompatibility can come about for two main reasons: either the assistive technology and the software package make competing demands on the resources of the student's computer, or the software package does not provide the 'hooks' needed for the assistive technology to interact with it.

Since the basic computing power and functionality of all components of the standard desktop computer are nowadays substantial, the first problem is less common. However one example of this type of problem is where the student uses a software-based speech synthesizer package that uses the computer's soundcard to produce the speech output as it 'reads aloud' the selected text. Some soundcards can only process one channel of audio at a time. Hence there may be a clash if the student is using the synthesizer to read text presented in a software package, but the same package is also trying to play audio messages.

One simple example of the second type of problem is where a student does not use a mouse or equivalent pointing device, and the controls of the software package are presented only for mouse interaction with no keyboard equivalents. There are more complex issues relating to whether a software package is compatible with accessibility functions in the operating system. These are commented on further in the section 'Software packages and educational multimedia' below.

When a computer is for a student's personal use, the best way of dealing with these problems is at the specification stage for the computer and the assistive technology (see below). These issues must also be considered when selecting software packages to be used as part of a course. If it is ensured that appropriate expertise is brought to bear at the time of specifying the student's computer and assistive technology, many of the problems caused by the first issue above can be averted. An important part of this process should be a review of the software packages students will require to use on their course(s). As a way of meeting its obligations to make its courses accessible to disabled students, an HEI should set essential accessibility criteria for selecting any software package for use in its courses as a matter of policy.

Solving these problems by correct specification is an ideal approach, but practical compatibility problems between particular assistive technologies and different software packages will still arise. Usually these can be worked round, but this often requires experience and technical skills. Educational establishments therefore need to make appropriate support staff available. This normally means equipping disabled student support teams with appropriate IT support skills, or ensuring that the main computer support teams include sufficient numbers of people with adequate expertise and experience relating to accessibility.

Assessing the needs of disabled students/ Disabled Student Allowances

The above overview of assistive technologies and approaches for making the computer accessible is intended only as a generic introduction. The selection of a particular piece of equipment to support an individual disabled student should be done in consultation with a suitably experienced needs assessor. In the UK, government grants entitled Disabled Students' Allowances (DSAs) are available to most disabled students in higher education. The equipment element of these grants includes a provision for assessment of need. Some universities offer their students support by providing needs assessments. Many such centres also offer these services to students from other institutions. The principal providers of needs assessments for equipment provided under the DSA scheme belong to the National Federation of Access Centres.[4]

Making the curriculum accessible

University education has, in some respects, changed little in terms of how it delivers the curriculum for hundreds of years. In most subject areas and institutions the lecture, seminar and tutorial remain the principal modes of delivery, with labs and fieldwork supplementing these, particularly in science and engineering subjects. However, even where these traditional approaches are maintained, computers are increasingly used to support them. A more comprehensive use of computers in delivering curricula is being adopted in some institutions that are seeking to make the Web central to their course delivery, in both campus-based and distance learning contexts. This is often achieved using commercial integrated suites of software called managed learning environments (MLE) or learning management systems (LMS). These combine administrative functions, such as course registration and student records, with mechanisms for creating and delivering Web-based courses. It is not the purpose of this book to comment upon the relative merits of the different ways of using computer technology in curriculum delivery. However it is a matter of fact that virtually all university courses use computers to a greater or lesser extent. This section gives some pointers to some actions that academics, programmers, Web authors and technical support teams can take to ensure that the computer-based aspects of their courses are accessible to disabled students.

In essence, making the computer-based elements of the curriculum accessible means:

1. Ensuring that the educational content is authored according to established accessibility guidelines.
2. Ensuring that the computer systems used to mediate this content to students are compatible with any assistive technology the students may need to use.
3. Further, where that content cannot be made accessible, making reasonable alternatives available.

The accessibility guidelines (referred to in point 1) are discussed further here, and referenced below. These guidelines essentially ensure that users can control to some extent the way content is presented to them, and that the delivery system can exploit the benefits of any assistive technology they elect to use. Hence, where earlier in this chapter pointers were given as to how a student can be enabled to use the computer, the following sections outline how those charged with delivering the curriculum should do so in a way that is accessible to students with disabilities.

Principles for accessibility

There exist some basic, well-established principles for accessibility that apply to all computer software. How these principles are realized in a particular piece of software or online content depends very much upon the authoring tools, programming language or development environment used. The choice of authoring environment can have a significant impact on how readily accessibility criteria are met.

General principles of software accessibility

- Allow for user customization (particularly of text size and style, background and foreground colours).
- Provide equivalent visual and auditory content and interface elements (text descriptions for images and video, transcription of auditory content, text labelling of interface elements, and so on).
- Provide compatibility with assistive technologies.
- Allow access to all functionality from keyboard alone (so that the software can be fully used without a mouse).
- Provide context and orientation information. (Support efficient navigation by informing users of where they are in a way that takes into account that some users may be using screen-readers).

WWW-based content and learning activities

The World Wide Web Consortium (W3C) creates Web standards. Under its Web Accessibility Initiative (WAI) it has drawn up extensive guidelines for creating Web pages that are accessible to many people with a disability. URLs to these and associated authoring and validation tools are given in the appendix to this chapter (Web accessibility guidelines). It should be noted that these are essentially guidelines to presenting information in an accessible way on the Web.

The WAI guidelines can certainly at first sight appear complex. A good starting point is WAI's own online training package, which they refer to as 'Curriculum', a reference to which is also in the Appendix. The WAI also provide a Techniques document and useful checklists for Web developers. There are 14 guidelines, each of which is associated with one or more checkpoints describing how to apply that guideline to particular features in Web pages. Each checkpoint is assigned one of three 'priority' levels, reflecting the impact not following it will have on accessibility. Levels of conformance are then specified against these priorities. It is recommended that an educational Web site seeking to meet the needs of disabled students should aim for 'Double-A' conformance, which means meeting all priority one and two checkpoints.

Most Web sites and pages are produced using authoring tools rather than 'hand crafting' HTML. There is a high degree of variability in how readily these tools support authoring in a way that conforms to the accessibility guidelines. However in response to US legislation, most of the major suppliers of such tools are seeking to address this in recent and planned releases.

Key principles to ensure accessibility when designing content for the WWW

- Follow the established standards and guidelines. This includes the standards for HTML as well as the Web Accessibility Guidelines. Text browsers or other assistive technology could misinterpret non-standard HTML.
- Keep designs clear and simple. This will promote the readability and usability of your pages. Good design for disabled people is good design for all!
- Test and validate your designs. This is preferably done by asking disabled people who use different ways of accessing the WWW to review your pages. Pages should at least be tested with a text browser and automatic validation tools.

It is important not merely to follow guidelines for accessibility when creating Web content, but then to test for accessibility. Ideally this is done by people with a range of disabilities viewing the pages with their usual assistive technology. Where this is not possible, however, there exist several automated validation tools available both for validating the HTML mark-up and for accessibility. Further, it is good standard practice to check Web pages with more than one browser. If a text-based browser is included in this procedure, key problems in accessibility can be detected. It is not usually good practice for Web developers lacking experience of accessibility to use some of the more sophisticated screen-readers intended for visually impaired people. Unless significant time is invested in learning and practising using these packages, problems with a Web site may be reported that are, in fact, owing to a lack of understanding of how to access the range of features of the screen-reader. The appendix to this chapter contains references to HTML and accessibility validators and some text browsers.

Issues for virtual learning environments

The use of integrated software suites to support and manage the learning process in higher education is gaining increasing prevalence. The terminology used here is various, and used in different ways by different communities. Broadly, however, the term virtual learning environment (VLE) refers to software that supports various online interactions between students and their tutors. The terms learning management system (LMS) or managed learning environment (MLE) are used to describe an integration of the whole range of information systems employed by an educational establishment. This may include a VLE as well as, for example, course registration and student record systems. Since this chapter is concerned with students' interaction with IT, the term VLE is used here.

A VLE usually provides access to the curriculum by providing a Web-publishing tool that enables tutors to present curriculum material (notes, presentations, assignments, reading lists, etc) to their students. This is normally combined with mechanisms to control when this material is made available to the students, and also to track their activity and progress. A VLE supports communication between students, their tutors and their peer-groups by, for example, e-mail conferences. The VLE also usually provides access to learning support material and services.

This brief statement of functionality of a VLE illustrates how the accessibility of a VLE has the potential to have a fundamental impact on the ability of students with disabilities to participate in courses using it. Since VLEs are designed to impact across the presentation of an entire course (and in some cases across an institution), tackling the accessibility issues in their use must be a strategic priority. The introduction of such a system that presents fundamental barriers to some disabled students would, without doubt, present significant problems for the institution in meeting its responsibilities under SENDA.

There are two broad areas for accessibility considerations in a VLE: access to and navigation around the student interface to the VLE itself, and access to content presented by the VLE. The first of these is an issue for the suppliers of the VLE. Indeed, all the major suppliers of VLEs are seeking to address the issues of accessibility in their products, mainly in response to the power of Section 508 of the Rehabilitation Act in the United States of America affecting universities' purchasing decisions. SENDA in the UK can also be reasonably expected to have a similar impact. If an HEI seeks to introduce a VLE, accessibility for disabled students to the facilities it provides should be a key feature of the specification used to evaluate the different packages available. Otherwise it could be judged to be signifi-cantly disadvantaging students with disabilities.

The second area of concern is that content presentation may also be affected by the design of a VLE, particularly with regard to the authoring tools it might offer teaching staff for creating content that will be presented to students via the VLE. These should ideally promote accessibility, and certainly not introduce barriers to disabled students. Much of the responsi-bility for the accessibility of the content will however fall on authors, who are usually the teaching staff. The task of authoring accessible content need not be an onerous one, but it is a key staff development issue. In most cases the content will consist of Web pages, so the accessibility issues outlined under WWW-based content and learning activities above apply. Much of the content will be text based and require little special response; however all teaching staff authoring content for presentation on a VLE need to be made aware of the accessibility issues, especially where they seek to include diagrams or multimedia elements.

Software packages and educational multimedia

Where institutions, departments or individual lecturers write, commission or purchase a piece of software to be used by students as part of their studies, they must, from the outset, specify the accessibility criteria and confirm that these are then met. It is far easier and less costly to incorporate accessibility features from the start, than to request 'fixes' once prototypes are in an advanced state of development. Typical examples of the sort of packages being considered here are simulations such as 'virtual science' packages, or computer programmes that offer students access to multimedia material. Provided the software used is accessible, the increasing use of computers in laboratory work has the potential to enable disabled students to be active participants rather than passive observers. Some universities have demonstrated the use of simulations and other computer-based activ-ities as alternatives to fieldwork that may otherwise have been inaccessible to some disabled students.

Java is currently a popular programming language for developing such educational software. Accessibility is achievable in Java programs, and pointers to developers' guidelines for achieving this are given in the appendix to this chapter. These guidelines direct the developer to program in such a way that the principles of accessibility given above are met. Following these guidelines may constrain a programmer to work in an unfamiliar way, particularly when creating user interfaces, and this may increase slightly the development time required. Helping the developer to understand why accessibility is important is, therefore, an integral part of the process of specifying and developing such software. Note that for some accessibility features, those requiring an integration of the software of the assistive technology and the Java program (such as screen-reader access to interface commands), the assistive technology must be produced in such a way as to enable this. This is increasingly the case with recent products, but it should be recognized that even if it is developed according to the Java accessibility guidelines, whether a piece of educational software is indeed accessible to disabled students may depend on the assisitive technology they employ.

Much educational software is developed not by programming as such, but by using multimedia authoring tools. Different tools promote, or even prevent, the creation of accessible educational software to differing degrees. It is beyond the scope of this chapter to survey these, and indeed this is a rapidly changing situation. Again, largely in response to US legislative pressure, many producers of these authoring environments are incorporating features to promote accessibility in recent versions of their products. It is important that the educator or institution commissioning software applications for students not only specifies the accessibility criteria, but also questions what development environment will be used and how this will enable the meeting of these criteria.

As in all other developments that are specified to be accessible, whether or not this is achieved should be tested for. Ideally this should be done as soon as early prototypes are available, as well as at the end of the development period. This will enable problems to be identified early and rectified.

Alternatives to print

The computer can prove an enabling technology for those who, for various reasons, find the use of printed material problematic or impossible. This can include those with a visual impairment or dyslexia, who have problems reading, or those whose physical disabilities make handling a book difficult. If set texts and other courseware normally presented in printed form can be made available electronically, these students can use their usual assistive technology to access them. The challenge for the curriculum providers is to make the appropriate texts available in a suitable electronic form. There are technical issues here, but copyright considerations in fact present some of the biggest barriers to exploiting this enabling opportunity. UK legislation currently in passage through Parliament (the Copyright (Visually Impaired Persons) Bill) is designed to remove many of these barriers. However it should be possible to make available electronically all texts specifically written for a course, and there are many text resources already available electronically. The emerging area of eBooks may be expected to accelerate the availability over the next few years, and this will then raise the issue of accessibility in eBook readers.

Educational assessment

Assessment of students' progress is a fundamental part of their participation in higher education. For disabled students it is important that they are assessed in a way that neither disadvantages them nor gives them an advantage over their peers. This is predominantly an issue of policy and good practice within the institution, and is outside the scope of this chapter. However two important areas relating to the use of IT by disabled students in examinations are briefly mentioned here.

Computers, assistive technology and examinations

First, it is important here to restate the individual nature of need. In examinations there is not one set response to facilitating all students with a similar disability; the best way to achieve this will, in fact, depend on the coping strategies they have developed individually. However where the normal coping strategies of particular disabled students relating to reading and writing include the use of a computer, this facility must also be extended to them in their examinations. If, for example, a blind student's preference is to use a computer with a screen-reader to access text and to write by typing, it would be appropriate to enable him or her to take the examination at a computer. There has been some reservation in the past about making computers available to students in examinations. An institution may wish to ensure that a student taking an exam at a computer has no access to information that would not normally be made available to others taking the same exam. This may mean providing a dedicated machine for the examinations that is not networked. Care must, however, be taken in such cases to ensure that any assistive technology the student normally uses is installed in this machine and configured as he or she would normally have it.

Computer-aided assessment

The second area to consider is the increasing use of computer-aided assessment (CAA) in higher education. Here students may undertake computer-based tests as preliminary assessments prior to taking a course, to provide them with feedback on progress, or as a summative assessment at the end of a course. Potentially CAA can enable many students with disabilities to be assessed in the same manner as their peers, which can help to reduce any feelings of special treatment. Clearly in order to achieve this, the presentation of the CAA tests must be compatible with any assistive technologies used. There is a wide variety of CAA systems used, some based on commercial products, while others are developed as bespoke solutions by particular institutions. However, virtually all of these use a Web-based approach for both the presentation of questions and the receiving of student responses. Hence the guidelines referred to above under WWW-based content and learning activities apply equally here. Particular care is needed when considering, for example, how a screen-reader user is able to navigate to the fields used to answer a given question. If check boxes are used to select from multiple choice answers, it must be clear which box refers to which answer in the way that the question is read out.

As in the case of VLEs discussed previously, clear accessibility criteria should be stated when an institution is considering purchasing or commissioning CAA software.

Conclusion

For many disabled people, computers are tools that enable them to participate in education, and they are being used increasingly in the delivery of the curriculum at higher education level. Subsequently, issues of access to computers and information technology must form a key part of policy and practice. These must be considered in the design of the curriculum, the way it is to be delivered and the provision of support services. These issues affect all teaching staff, and many with roles in management, strategic planning, and service provision within higher education.

This chapter has set out to inform the development of policy and practice in this area. It has provided an introduction to how disabled people may be enabled to make effective use of computers. It has gone on to give an overview of the implications of the differing ways the computer may be used for meeting the needs of disabled students in higher education. Universities in the UK now have a legal as well as moral obligation not to discriminate against students on the grounds of their disability. In nearly all cases, enabling disabled students access to computer-mediated services and elements of the curriculum falls within the description of reasonable adjustment used in this legislation.

Acknowledgements

Thanks to many people who have informed my understanding of the practical issues of assistive technology and software accessibility over the last 15 years, and in particular to my colleagues in the Accessible Educational Media group at the Open University for their assistance in writing this chapter. Special thanks are owed to Dr Chetz Colwell who contributed to key areas of this chapter, and together with Dr Hazel Kennedy, made suggestions for improvements to the text.

Appendix of online resources
Web accessibility guidelines and tools

URLs to the WC3's Web Accessibility Initiative's guidelines and associated tools, etc are listed here.

WAI content guidelines

Guidelines: http://www.w3.org/TR/WAI-WEBCONTENT/
Techniques: http://www.w3.org/TR/WAI-WEBCONTENT-TECHS/
Checklists: http://www.w3.org/TR/WAI-WEBCONTENT/full-check-list.html
Curriculum: http://www.w3.org/WAI/wcag-curric/

Accessibility validators

Bobby: http://www.cast.org/bobby/
A-Prompt: http://www.aprompt.ca/

W3C validation services

For HTML validation: http://validator.w3.org/
For CSS validation: http://jigsaw.w3.org/css-validator/

HTML Tidy repair tool

The following tool helps in 'cleaning up' non-standard HTML sometimes created by authoring tools:
http://www.w3.org/People/Raggett/tidy/

Text browsers

Opera: http://www.opera.com/
Lynx: http://lynx.browser.org/

Other resources

TechDis

TechDis is a Joint Information Systems Committee (JISC) funded service supporting the further and higher education community in all aspects of technology and disabilities and/or learning difficulties. Its WWW home page can be found at http://www.techdis.ac.uk/

DISinHE

DISinHE was the predecessor of TechDis and is no longer an ongoing project but many of its online resources are still available including guidelines for accessible courseware, available at: http://www.disinhe.ac.uk/library/article.asp?id=24

As an appendix to the above, a useful courseware design checklist: http://www.disinhe.ac.uk/library/chapter.asp?id=72

BECTa

BECTa (British Educational Communications and Technology Agency) is primarily focused at the schools/FE sectors. It provides good information sheets on the use of information and communications technology by students with disabilities: http://www.becta.org.uk/technology/infosheets/index.html

Microsoft

Microsoft provides guidelines on incorporating accessibility features into applications for a range of disabilities. This information is included in the MSDN (Microsoft Developers Network) Library under 'User Interface Design and Development – Accessibility': http://msdn.microsoft.com/library/default.asp

IBM

IBM has an Accessibility Centre that, among other things, hosts fairly detailed information for software developers together with a software accessibility checklist: http://www-3.ibm.com/able/accesssoftware.html

JAVA accessibility

Accessibility guidelines, tutorials and tools for developers working in JAVA are made available by SUN Microsystems at http://www.sun.com/access/developers/index.html

IBM provide a developers guide and checklist at http://www-3.ibm.com/able/snsjavag.html

http://www-3.ibm.com/able/accessjava.html

Dyslexia

The British Dyslexia Association (BDA) publishes a large number of leaflets including some on computing and students with dyslexia: http://www.bda-dyslexia.org.uk/

Dyslexic.com is a commercial concern that aims to be the UK's one-stop-shop to meet the technology needs of dyslexic people of all ages. It provides some useful resources including issues of accessibility to the WWW for people with dyslexia: http://www.dyslexic.com/rational.htm

Visual impairment

The Royal National Institute for the Blind (RNIB) produces its own notes on accessible Web design, largely based on the W3C guidelines. Available at http://www.rnib.org.uk/digital/hints.htm

Notes

1. Martyn Cooper is contactable at the Institute of Educational Technology, Open University, Walton Hall, Milton Keynes MK7 6AA. E-mail: m.cooper@open.ac.uk
2. Text of SENDA: http://www.legislation.hmso.gov.uk/acts/acts2001/20010010.htm
3. See http://www.nctd.org.uk/
4. See http://www.nfac.org.uk/
5. See http://www.parliament.the-stationery-office.co.uk/pa/cm200102/cmbills/023/2002023.htm

Part three

Visual and auditory impairments: physical disability

4

Supporting deaf students in higher education

Joy Jarvis and Pamela Knight

Introduction

The students on the art course were to undertake research on an individually chosen artist for discussion in a seminar group the following week. The deaf student in the group worked hard to produce material on his chosen subject, 'Constable'. It was only when he came to present his material that he discovered that the spoken instructions for the task had been, 'Choose a portrait artist ...'

More and more deaf students are entering higher education institutions and following courses alongside their hearing peers. This means that it is likely that lecturers in HE will have a deaf student in their class at some time in their teaching. Providing equality of access to the content of courses and to all the facilities and potential gains of higher education requires appropriate support systems. It also requires awareness and skills on the part of academic, research and support staff who deliver the courses and on the part of hearing student peers. As shown in the example above, even missing one word in an instruction can mean the difference between success and failure.

This chapter looks at issues for deaf students in a higher education context, and ways in which identifiable needs can be met by staff and institutions. While deaf students are all individuals, there are a number of issues that may be common to all, to a greater or lesser extent, and a range of strategies is available which can be tailored to meet individual needs.

Issues for deaf students

Linguistic issues

A common factor for all deaf students is that they have a degree of hearing loss significant enough to affect, or to have affected, their development of spoken language. It is known that hearing loss in itself does not affect the inherent ability to develop a language. The problem is that hearing loss or deafness means that access to language is inhibited to a greater or lesser degree. Language development is therefore restricted by that lack of access to the spoken word. The degree of loss can vary between a mild, moderate, severe and profound loss (for further details see Tate-Maltby and Knight, 2000). In very general terms, students with a hearing loss that falls into the mild, moderate or severe category will, with the assistance of hearing aids and appropriate teaching and support, develop spoken language as a first or preferred language. Their language development may be delayed or limited, but it will be the language in which they function to their fullest capacity. These students may also have developed some sign language skills for social interaction with other deaf peers. Students whose deafness falls into the profound category are likely to have developed sign language as a first or preferred language and English as a second language, which may well be written and not spoken English.

The first and preferred language choice will also have been affected by the type of education the student has had prior to entering higher education. Students with more residual hearing are likely to have been educated in an aural/oral environment where spoken English is the medium of instruction. Students with less hearing are likely to have been educated in a total communication or bilingual setting, where sign language will have been the language of instruction and English the language of literacy. Focusing on preferred language use leads us to the premise that deaf students can be identified as differing linguistic groups: those for whom spoken language is a first or preferred language and those for whom sign language is a first language (for further information see Gregory *et al*, 1998). The implications for curriculum delivery and support are different for the two groups. For one the support will need to be for oral delivery of courses, while for the other, emphasis will need to be on interpreting the curriculum into sign language. Both groups, however, will need other, similar types of support in relation to aspects such as assessment and access to facilitative teaching styles.

Previous educational experience

As with all students, deaf students will come from a wide variety of educational settings, and so bring to higher education a diversity of learning experiences and knowledge of ways of learning. In a special school for deaf pupils, students will have been mainly within a deaf environment, and are likely to have been in very small classes, allowing for specialist teaching and individual support. A mainstream school that has identified provision for deaf pupils will have provided a peer group of deaf students within an ordinary school, appropriate support within the classroom, and also pre and post lesson tutoring as necessary. Many deaf students with English as their first language will have been individually included in their local mainstream school, with minimal support from an advisory teacher whose role will have been to advise mainstream teachers on appropriate strategies to use with their deaf pupils.

These different placements may well have influenced the individual's ability to learn independently. Many students will be aware of their own support needs, and may be proactive in this regard. Others may have experienced a support system which has created a certain dependency, and they may not be aware of their needs in different educational contexts and how these needs can be met effectively.

> I was used to being in a very small group at school and having a teacher around me all the time ... it was different at uni.
>
> (Comment from a student)

> I indicated to the university that no support was necessary. After four terrible weeks at the start of my course I knew this was wrong. I could not understand many of the lecturers and was unable to cope with group work. It took several months to organize the appropriate help for me.
>
> (Nottingham Trent, 1995: 8)

Understanding and use of English

As has been noted, for many deaf students English is a second or even a third language, or is a language that they have acquired more slowly and with greater difficulty than hearing students. They have more limited input when they are learning the language, as access to the sound of speech may be very limited, speech reading (lip reading) is difficult and never completely accurate, and there is no opportunity to access what has not been said directly to you, so there is no information from 'overhearing' others or from media such as radio and television. Certain features of English are difficult to identify without hearing, such as the speech sound 's' which often carries grammatical information about person, plurality or possession. Because of their limited access to English, deaf students may have a less rich vocabulary base than hearing students, although many deaf young people and adults read avidly and acquire much of their knowledge of English through print. Deaf students in higher education generally have a good understanding of English, although there may be 'gaps' in their knowledge of vocabulary, and there could be misunderstandings over terminology, particularly when words can have multiple meanings.

All these factors make it likely that some deaf students will have more difficulty accessing academic language, both in sessions and in texts, than hearing students. One deaf student noted in relation to his lecturers' use of English and to the language of texts used on the course: 'It is too high a level of English with too many sophisticated words.' He also felt that he needed more guidance on how to use the suggested reading, feeling swamped by lists of books and articles and unsure how to tackle them, particularly as he felt that he read more slowly than other students. Many students, not just those who are deaf, would find technical glossaries, clear definitions of new terms and an explanation of subject specific language helpful.

Interviews

Before students enter an institution of higher education they may need to attend an interview. In order to provide for equality of opportunity for deaf applicants to demonstrate their knowledge and abilities, their needs, particularly for appropriate communication, need to be identified.

Individual interviews

Prior to the interview it is important to establish the applicant's communication needs. The use of fax or a text phone can enable communication to take place before the interview. In some cases the admission form may just state that the student is 'deaf', without giving further information. In other cases admissions staff may assume that a deaf person needs an interpreter, which may not be the case. Many deaf applicants will not understand British Sign Language, so an interpreter would not necessarily be appropriate provision.

If it is established that an interpreter is needed, one should be booked by the institution in advance (the RNID information line can give details, see p 76). When an applicant is interviewed using an interpreter, it is important that the interviewer talks to the applicant, not the interpreter. If an interpreter is not being used and the interview is conducted orally, then lip reading and listening conditions need to be good. This includes arranging a quiet environment with the interviewer sitting in good light, but not with his/her back to the light. Clear speech that is not exaggerated or too loud will make comprehension easier, but it is vital that the interviewer checks what has been understood by the applicant. The applicant may think he or she has understood what has been said, but a slight mishearing can alter the message. Distinguishing between the words 'must' and 'mustn't', for example, may be impossible for the deaf person without some additional context or information, and may lead to complete misunderstanding. The RNID publication *The Access Guide* (2001) gives a clear description of good ways of communicating effectively in a one to one context with a deaf person.

Group interviews

For some courses group, rather than individual, interviews are used. This may be so that skills such as working with others can be observed and assessed. Interviews for prospective teachers, for example, can involve individual interviews, a test to check the use of written English, and group activities to assess communication, co-operation and presentation skills, all of which could be seen as essential for entrants to a teaching course. For deaf applicants group interviews need to be planned carefully to ensure that they can demonstrate their skills and are not disadvantaged by being unable to follow what is being said by other group members. Seating needs to be arranged so that all the candidates can see each other, and group communication procedures need to be established in relation to the individual candidates' needs. These are likely to include ensuring that candidates do not talk at the same time, that people indicate when they are about to speak so that the deaf candidate can locate and speech read the speaker, and ensuring that people do not obscure their mouths when speaking. Pace needs to allow for ample time for processing information and for the interpreter, if there is one, to sign all contributions. If small group activities are to be observed and assessed, communication needs within the group need to be identified, and the activity should be undertaken in a context with limited background noise.

Types of support

Once students have been accepted onto a course their needs should be identified and support arranged. Each student will need a different support package, and the student, working together with the staff involved and relevant disability services, should be able to identify initial requirements and then modify support arrangements in the light of experience.

Support comes in three forms:

- human resources;
- technical aids;
- advice on teaching styles and useful strategies.

All of the above aim to maximize the learning opportunities for deaf students. Harrington (1998) describes the function of support as the media through which the educational content must pass to meet the mind of the deaf student. The individual support programme devised from this provision will depend upon the individual needs of each student. The type of support will depend largely upon the first or preferred language of the student and upon his or her individual learning style.

The following are examples of the types of support offered to a student, and their role in maximizing the student's ability to access the message of the lecturer and the classroom.

Human resources

Note takers

The note taker's role is to channel information given by the lecturer or other contributors from spoken English to written English notes. It is effectively transliteration, and in theory the note taker needs no previous knowledge of the subject area. A note taker allows the student to concentrate on listening and on observing the lip patterns of the lecturer, which are an important element in their comprehension of spoken English. The note taker needs to be aware of the learning style of the student, and to take notes that match this, are comprehensive and do not 'filter' information.

> It really helps to have knowledge of the subject and to work consistently with the same lecturers ... it also helps to have access to the lecture notes beforehand so that I know what will be happening. ... I try to give all the content but I do use diagrams and arrows and things like that because it seems to help deaf students ... oh and coloured pens as well.
>
> (Comment from a note taker)

Lip speakers

A lip speaker will sit directly in front of the student and remouth the message as it comes from the lecturer. Again it is a simple transliteration, and in theory needs no knowledge of the subject. However many lip speakers report that a previous knowledge of the content of any session is a help.

It is also likely that some of the presented content will be missed, as it is virtually impossible to keep up with all information given. There are also problems during discussions or when two people are talking at the same time.

Speech to text operator

This performs a similar function in that it is a transliteration of the lecture content and can be used as note taking. It is possible for the student to read the text on a screen, as it is typed by a trained operator. (The RNID has an information leaflet.) An example of available software is Stereotype (available from Sheffield Hallam University Press, see p 76). This requires two computers, one which is used by an operator who types text as it is spoken, often using pre-programmed abbreviations, and the other which shows the text on a screen for the deaf student. The screen is split, with a space for the student to type notes. Text can be saved in a normal word processing package and edited by the student as appropriate.

All the above support staff come into the category of 'monolingual' support workers. That is, they are working within the same language as the delivery of the lecture or seminar, but in a different mode. The language is changed from a spoken form into English notes, lip patterns or typed onto a keyboard. It is not expected that any of these support workers will be involved in interaction in the classroom or the content of lectures.

Sign language interpreters

Sign language interpreting functions within a bilingual setting, where the language of delivery is being translated into a second language. The interpreter's role is to translate from the spoken language of delivery into sign language, and be prepared to translate what is offered by the student in sign language back into spoken English. An interpreter has to be familiar with the subject content in order to translate it effectively into a second language. In this case, a previous knowledge and understanding of the subject matter is of paramount importance to the interpreter if he or she is to give full information to the students.

It is vital that students and lecturers are 'deaf aware' in that they understand the conventions of working with an interpreter ... where there is specialist subject matter it is crucial to have access to the content in order to ensure that I know all the relevant signs.

(Comments from an interpreter)

Technical aids

Hearing aids

Technical aids, that is hearing aids, generally come in two forms. The first is a hearing aid worn entirely by the student, and the second is a radio aid, where the microphone is worn by the lecturer and the receiver by the student. The function of both systems is to amplify and clarify sound. Providing all the equipment is appropriately set up and in good working order, it should do this reasonably efficiently. Students in higher education should be entirely responsible for the use and maintenance of their own hearing aids and radio systems, and will be responsible for all parts including the microphone, which they should pass to the lecturer at the start of each class. The lecturer needs to wear the microphone near the top of his/her chest and remember to switch it on.

Unlike glasses, hearing aids do not 'correct' or restore normal hearing, but can only 'aid' to a greater or lesser degree the residual hearing of the deaf student. While a hearing aid can do much to enhance the listening experience of the deaf student, there are also limitations to its functioning. (For further reading see Tate-Maltby and Knight, 2000.)

The main limitation is that, unlike the human ear, the aid is not as yet able to discriminate between the sounds of speech and ongoing background noise. They are both amplified similarly. This has implications for the noise level in the classroom, as well as external factors such as buildings with busy corridors and situated close to traffic noise. A further implication for aids worn entirely by the student is that the efficiency of the aid decreases dramatically with increased distance from the source of sound.

Students with hearing aids may also be at a disadvantage when there is more than one source of speech within the room. Here the microphone needs to be handed round to each speaker in turn. A conference microphone, centrally placed, can help this situation within small groups. All this of course alters the dynamics of the classroom, and the spontaneity and flow of a class can be interrupted. It is hard to see how this can be avoided if deaf students are to have equal access to the learning experience.

Sound systems

This is basically a miniature public address system for the classroom, where there are a microphone, an amplifier and a series of loudspeakers positioned at suitable points around the room. The aim of the system is to ensure that sound is radiated as evenly as possible around the room, and deaf students are not disadvantaged by distance from the source of sound. The implications for lecturers are that they need to be aware of efficient microphone use, particularly in a group discussion or question and answer session.

Advice on teaching styles and useful strategies for lecturers

In every higher education institution there is an officer organizing advice and support for students with disabilities, including deaf students. One of his/her roles is to offer advice to lecturers about appropriate teaching strategies. Deaf awareness sessions may be provided, which are likely to include information on the needs of deaf learners, and ways in which these can be met in different educational contexts. The use of technical aids will be explained, and the roles of different support workers and how all can work effectively together will be explored. Often these sessions are run by deaf professionals.

> As with the general public, few lecturers have been involved with deaf people at all and these sessions are often the first time they have met professional deaf people ... we have really positive feedback from those who come to our INSET sessions. ... I just wish that is was compulsory for all lecturers.
> (Comments from a disability officer)

Students too would benefit from deaf awareness. One deaf student noted, 'It was difficult in discussions etc with other students who were not deaf aware.' Most importantly, all hearing staff involved with deaf students need to have an insight into the history and culture of deaf people. Deaf students, seen as a linguistic group, have a language, community and culture of their own which they bring to the university setting. This should be understood, appreciated and seen as a valuable addition to student life.

Student scenarios

In the complex and varied experiences of life in a higher education institution, the deaf student will encounter many new situations. These will include teaching and learning situations such as lectures, seminars and workshops, as well as small group tutorials, individual study time and work experiences. Each situation presents its own particular difficulties and challenges for the deaf student, and throws up subtle differences for support.

Lectures

My most immediate problem was being unable to follow what was said at lecturers and seminars.

(Rees, 1983: 156)

The main feature of effective communication with deaf people is visual communication. Whether deaf students have a spoken or signed language as their first or preferred language, the importance of clear and continual visual access to the speaker or interpreter cannot be over-emphasized. Difficulties come when students do not have this access. This means that students must, at all times, have good sight of the lecturer and most importantly his/her face and lips. This has practical implications for such things as moustaches and beards which may conceal the mouth, turning around to write on a black/white board while still talking, and walking around the room. If lecturers stand with their back to a bright light source, this can also throw their face into shadow and be uncomfortable for the deaf student.

The physical setting, such as poor lighting and poor acoustics, can also produce difficulties. The facility for students to seat themselves comfortably, so that they are near enough to the source of sound (the lecturer) to receive a good clear acoustic signal but not so near that it becomes a strain to see them, is important.

Technical aids, such as video, use of OHPs and PowerPoint presentations, are excellent visual resources for deaf students, but lowering of lights, for example, may enhance the viewing for hearing students but severely disadvantage the deaf student. It is salutary to consider how much information one would obtain from a video without a soundtrack. Many deaf students will not be able to understand a video unless it is subtitled. If this is not possible, a transcript beforehand is helpful, and/or the opportunity to borrow the video and look at it with hearing peers on another occasion. It is also important in a lecture context that verbal information is not given simultaneously with visual material. It is very tempting for the lecturer to talk about the text while it is moving on the screen, or to comment while pointing to an example on a slide, but the deaf student cannot watch the screen and the lecturer or the interpreter at the same time. If an interpreter is interpreting the lecture, ideally s/he will have been given the lecture notes in advance so that key vocabulary and concepts can be identified. Time will need to be given for the interpreter to complete the signing of one section of the lecture before moving onto the next part. Appropriate strategies used by the lecturer can lead to improved access to the lecture.

> The lecturer was great. He always made sure that I was looking at him and gave me time to read anything before he started talking again ... it really helped.
>
> (Student comment)

Seminars

When students are together in group tutorials, seminars or workshops they are likely to be undertaking collaborative work. This generally involves discussions in groups, sharing ideas and feeding back key points to the whole group. The outcome will be both in the process of learning, how one engages with the material, and also in the product, whereby new ideas and information will have been acquired. These are clearly key aspects of learning to which deaf students require access. For the deaf student, however, a group context will be much more difficult than an individual discussion, or even a lecture context where one speaker only is involved. The deaf student may find that conversation from other groups is amplified by a hearing aid and effectively masks what members of his/her own group are saying. When contributions are made by many people, the deaf student will take time to locate who is speaking, and by then much of the information for speech reading will have been lost. In discussions people talk at the same time, interrupt, and conversational turns move rapidly, making it impossible for the deaf person to follow the conversation. One deaf student who was undertaking a graphic design course reported:

> I'm fine talking with one person provided I can lip read. They understand me too and there is no problem. In one to one conversations with my tutor I was OK. The problem was that they didn't realize that the whole situation was different in a group. I just didn't know what was going on.
>
> (Student comment)

Other students noted the same thing: 'From time to time there were groups of students discussing various things. I missed the information.' Some tutors also felt that deaf students were having problems in this context. One noted, 'The key problem was discussion/workshops. It was hard for them to participate.'

Deaf students can participate if they know what is being said by everyone else. This is easier to ensure if one person is leading the discussion. A tutor, for example, may ask an initial question to which some group members will respond. If the tutor then repeats back or summarizes each contribution, the deaf person will have more chance of knowing what has been said. If an interpreter is involved, time needs to be allowed for him/her to sign what has been said. Once the students are put into smaller groups, the participants need to use certain strategies that will help the deaf student to participate. This includes having as quiet an environment as possible; arranging chairs and other furniture so that everyone can see each other; speakers looking at the deaf person to allow for speech reading; pausing for the interpreter as appropriate; and using a conference micro- phone in the middle of the group to allow the voices of all participants to be heard more clearly. Probably the most difficult of these strategies is for speakers to look at the deaf person rather than talk to the group in general, but once they realize the difference this can make to supporting the deaf person's participation, students are often able to do this well, and eventually do it as a matter of course.

These strategies are not always easy to use, however.

> We always start well, but then the session moves along rapidly and we forget. I know that [the deaf student] missed out.
>
> (Tutor comment)

For tutors, remembering that they have a deaf student in the group can be an issue, and this needs to be resolved in some way. Often the student needs to remind the tutor. 'I liked it when he gave me the microphone because then I remembered he was in the group.' For hearing students there may be issues in working in a group with deaf students. One tutor felt that some hearing students found it 'a very positive experience and a number of [them] tried to develop their own understanding of British Sign Language' while another tutor on the same course reported: 'Some students found it tiresome to work with them as it slowed the pace.' The speed of the session is very likely to be an issue, as by pausing, repeating and if necessary clari- fying information, the pace will be slowed.

Students undertaking courses involving work placements

A number of deaf students will be undertaking professional courses that involve placements in work contexts outside the university. Provision for deaf students to have equal opportunities in these different settings requires liaison between the university and the placement setting, and an awareness of the needs of deaf people on the part of all involved. For the purposes of this chapter, teachers in training will be used as an example of how issues can be identified and dealt with by the student and the institutions involved.

Teachers in training

There is an increasing, although still small, number of deaf teachers working both in mainstream schools and, after additional training, in provisions for deaf children. Student teachers are required to spend a significant proportion of their time on the course working in schools. For deaf students there will be a range of issues here, from communicating with staff and pupils to knowing when the end of a lesson is being signalled by a bell. There may be lack of deaf awareness on the part of the school staff, who may be concerned about how a deaf person can manage and ensure the safety of a group of children in addition to teaching them.

The key aspect is for the people involved, including the student, to work together to identify the student's strengths and how any issues can be managed. Students and school contexts are very different, so there is no one model of the best way to ensure that deaf students have the opportunity to develop and demonstrate their teaching skills. Strategies can include placing deaf students where there is a resourced unit for deaf pupils or where deaf children are individually included in mainstream classes, so that staff and pupils are 'deaf aware'. Equipment is important, such as a pager to alert the student to the end of the lesson or to the fire alarm. Particular strategies need to be devised by individual students and staff. One deaf student found it hard to hear contributions from quieter children in whole-class sessions, and devised a system whereby two children were identified as 'listeners' for the day. They had the responsibility of repeating children's contributions if requested to do so. They saw this as a responsible job, and it also encouraged them to listen carefully to their peers. Deaf people often use visual scanning to see what is going on around them as they are not alerted to environmental changes by sound. Student teachers can use this very effectively in classroom contexts. Individual students can, with support from staff, identify appropriate strategies to meet the needs of all involved, strategies that they can continue to use and develop when they start in their first teaching post.

Assessment

Assessment is a very important aspect of university life. The example at the beginning of the chapter, of the art student who misheard the instructions for a task, demonstrates the importance of all tasks being clarified with the student and preferably being given in writing. Often important assessment tasks are given on handouts or in course booklets, but supplementary information may be given orally and may be missed by the deaf student.

Assessment tasks are often written, but may include other aspects such as presentations or practical projects. Most assessments involve some writing, even if it is just a summary of the key points of a presentation, although often, of course, an academic essay is expected. Some deaf students, particularly perhaps those with English as a second language, may have problems expressing themselves effectively in written English. They may miss out parts of speech, write sentences which appear 'odd' or use vocabulary inappropriately.

Lecturers working with a group of students that included two sign language users were asked about their students' written assignments in relation to those of the hearing students. Their responses suggested that there were issues with some aspects of grammar, but that the demonstration of knowledge of the topic was not affected by this.

> There were some problems with written English. Conversations with [the faculty co-ordinator for students with disabilities] suggested that these were related to deafness. There was little impeding of meaning overall.
>
> (Comment by course tutor)

A key point therefore in assessment is to mark for content, unless the use of English is part of the assessment criteria. Some deaf students would benefit from additional English courses, similar to those offered to students from overseas, or from courses in academic writing. At some institutions there is support available specifically for deaf students, which is undertaken by lecturers qualified in this field.

Other forms of assessment, such as presentations, may enable the student to demonstrate his/her knowledge without worrying about written English. If clarity of speech is an issue, the student may prefer to use an interpreter to 'voice over' his/her signed presentation.

Individual support

Ideally the deaf student will have additional time, as an individual or in a very small group, to check understanding of course material and to identify any issues arising in relation to the subjects being studied. If these tutorials are undertaken by the course tutor, it gives him/her a good idea of the level of understanding of course members, and this can help with planning future sessions.

Summary of issues

This chapter has considered many of the issues related to ensuring that deaf students have equal access to the academic courses offered to them in higher education institutions. It is important that lecturers do gain an awareness and understanding of deaf issues and deaf culture, but in reality this takes time and an ongoing interest. The likely scenario for lecturers, in this culture of modularization, is that they have a deaf student for a semester only or in a tutorial group occasionally, and the opportunity to develop understanding and strategies fully is not possible.

While there is no intention to trivialize the issues, there are nevertheless many teaching points that could be highlighted and integrated immediately into teaching styles, which would enhance the learning experience for the deaf student. These are summarized below.

Key points for lecturers to consider
1   Students
- Consult with the student about his/her own needs.
- Ensure other students in the group are aware of the issues.
- Ensure the student can lip read you effectively at all times.

2   Other professionals
- Be aware of the strategies required when working alongside note takers, interpreters and communication support workers.
- Be clear about the role of other professionals working alongside in the classroom.

3   Technical aids
- Remember that the greater the distance the hearing aid wearer is from the sound source, the less s/he will hear.
- Try to reduce background noise.
- Remember to switch on the microphone if one is used.

4   *Teaching strategies*

- Repeat and rephrase information.
- Use visual resources.
- Repeat answers back to the group.
- Do not offer two modes of communication at the same time, such as speech and visual information.

Conclusion

This chapter has dealt largely with academic inclusion, and ensuring that deaf students have equal access with their hearing peers to the academic content of the courses they have chosen to follow. Of course this is important, and in many ways it is central to the experience of higher education. However higher education offers a much broader scenario to the student than academic access and subsequent success.

The term used for this broader scenario is social inclusion. Research has indicated that deaf students in inclusive education, whether it is secondary, further or higher education, perform relatively well academically but report feeling socially and emotionally isolated (Foster, 1988) and finding it difficult to establish their own identity as a deaf student (Ladd, 1991).

Social inclusion is hard to define. It has been summarized by Powers (1996) as an attitude and not a place. It is primarily related to the 'ethos' of the whole establishment that is welcoming, open and has appropriate strategies in place to access all aspects of life in a higher education context. This is a clear aim for all establishments. Deafness is largely a linguistic issue, and language and communication are central to social inclusion. For those deaf students with an effective command of spoken language, inclusion alongside hearing students is possible, although, as previously suggested in this chapter, many oral deaf students also have well-developed sign language skills. Even though many deaf students have good oral skills and can communicate effectively with hearing students, it is evident that the opportunity to mix with a deaf peer group for relaxed communication is essential for the emotional and social well-being of many deaf students.

This of course poses a problem for institutions of higher education, as indeed it does for mainstream schools. It leads to the concept of particular universities becoming centres for deaf students, as has happened at the University of Central Lancashire and others. Here a significant number of deaf students on the campus means that support resources can be pooled, deaf awareness can be strongly promoted, and deaf students are ensured of a deaf peer group. If the number of deaf students in a university is very small, it seems that academic support can be given but social inclusion may be more difficult to attain. But clearly if universal inclusion is accepted as our goal, such difficulties must be overcome. Establishing an inclusive ethos within a group can help a great deal and is a small, but significant, step towards the deaf student being fully included in the university community.

> I have a deaf student in my group of 30. I asked her to explain her needs to the group and she did this very clearly. One thing she said was that she would like a fellow student to take notes for her. After she had finished talking, I said that anyone who was interested in helping with note taking could stay behind and everyone else could go for coffee-break. No one left to go to coffee.
>
> (Comment from tutor)

References

Foster, S (1988) Life in the mainstream: Reflections of deaf college freshmen on their experiences in the mainstreamed high school, *Journal of Rehabilitation of the Deaf*, **22**, pp 37–56

Gregory, S, Knight, P, McCracken, W, Powers, S, and Watson, L (1998) *Issues in Deaf Education*, David Fulton, London

Harrington, F J (1998) Deaf students and the interpreted classroom: the effect of translation on education, in *The Accessible Millennium: Developing policy and provision for disabled students in higher education*, ed A Hurst and G Gagliano, Ashgate Press, Aldershot

Ladd, P (1991) Making plans for Nigel: an erosion of identity by mainstreaming, in *Being Deaf: The experience of deafness*, ed G Taylor and J Bishop, Open University, Buckingham

Nottingham Trent University (1995) *Access and Communication Support for Deaf and Hearing Impaired Students in Higher Education*, Nottingham Trent University Press, Nottingham

Powers, S (1996) Inclusion is an attitude, not a place, Parts I and II, *Journal of the British Association of Teachers of the Deaf*, 20, pp 35–41 and 30, pp 65–69

Rees, J (1983) *Sing a Song of Silence: A deaf girl's odyssey*, Futura, London

Royal National Institute for Deaf People (RNID) (2001) *The Access Guide*, RNID, London

Tate-Maltby, M and Knight, P (2000) *Audiology: An introduction for teachers and other professionals*, David Fulton, London

Other sources of information

British Association of Teachers of the Deaf
Web site: www.batod.org.uk

Connevans Ltd
54 Albert Rd North, Reigate
Surrey RG2 9YR
(audiological equipment)

Forest Bookshop
Web site: www.ForestBooks.com
(books, videos, CD ROMs on deafness and deaf issues)

National Deaf Children's Society
Web site: www.ndcs.org.uk

P C Werth Ltd
Audiology House, 45 Nightingale Lane
London SW12 8SP
(audiological equipment)

Royal National Institute for Deaf People (2001) *Education Guidelines Project: Deaf Students in Further Education*, RNID, London

Royal National Institute for Deaf People
Web site: www.rnid.org.uk
Tel: 0808 808 0123
Textphone: 0808 808 9000

Sheffield Hallam University Press
The Learning Centre, City Campus
Sheffield S11WB
(for 'Stereotype' computer software)

5

Students with visual impairment

Archie W N Roy

Introduction

Recent evidence from a number of sources indicates that visually impaired students access and succeed in almost all higher education curriculum areas as defined by the Higher Education Statistics Agency. Much of this data comes from students who formally declare serious sight loss as a disability to their universities and colleges (Richardson and Roy, 2002) while some comes from the voluntary sector, supporting visually impaired students who may not necessarily choose to disclose loss of sight formally (Simkiss, Garner and Dryden, 1998). Just about all broad subject areas are accessed now, and generally, visual impairment does not have a significantly negative effect on level of attainment as defined by classification of degrees awarded by institutions of higher education.

However, representation of visually impaired students across subjects of study is skewed differently than that of higher education students with no reported disability, and also differently than all students. Some subjects of study have tended to attract visually impaired students more (such as computer science, social studies and humanities), others less (such as architecture, education, and subjects allied to medicine). To some extent, this has to do with factors that will have less impact on course selection currently and in future. For instance, it is very likely that representation of visually impaired students will increase in education, since student selection guidelines issued by the General Teaching Council and similar bodies have recently become much more inclusive. Knowledge of this will affect visually impaired school-leavers and adult returners when they weigh up possible course options. Yet some subjects of study impose specific challenges which staff and students need to overcome.

Inclusive learning practice begins pre-entry at the guidance, admissions and assessment stage. Higher education staff are increasingly moving away, fortunately, from any tendency to use stereotyped views to 'steer' visually impaired students into the more traditional areas of learning associated with them in the past. At the same time, this poses challenges for staff who are keen to offer visually impaired students a genuinely equal opportunity to access learning in curriculum areas that can be very visual. Visually impaired students should be listened to: they can speak directly from their own experiences, their learning strategies employed at school, college and in daily life. They are innovative. They have had to be to progress on into higher education.

Creativity and innovation by staff are also now becoming very important issues. The responsibility, however, is a shared one. Academic teaching staff should make good use of internal and external academic colleagues whose expertise lies in disability and curriculum development (see for example SHEFC, 2000). External bodies in the voluntary sector such as Royal National Institute for the Blind (RNIB) are additional useful contacts and have considerable experience to offer. The goal is to remove the ingrained and longstanding barriers to learning faced by visually impaired students.

Defining visual impairment

In brief, the term 'visual impairment' covers a wide range of degrees and types of sight loss. A visually impaired student's functional vision for purposes of study can, depending on the individual, range from no useful sight (such as complete sight loss or light perception only) to useful partial sight. The term 'blindness' itself is used to cover a range of eye conditions up to about 3/60 visual loss against the ophthalmic Snellen chart. A definition of blindness reached by this means is used for registration purposes. The actual description of '3/60 vision' means that the student is seeing at 3 metres a letter that would be visible at 60 metres to someone else with 20/20 visual acuity. The term 'partial sight' has a formal definition of between 3/60 and 6/60 vision.

A student may well be a relative expert on the eye condition itself and be able to explain to staff the precise cause and nature of sight loss from within the vast array of possible conditions. For some students though, particularly those undergoing medical examinations to investigate recent sight loss, there may be no existing diagnosis or prognosis. Some students may also not have had the condition clearly explained to them. Again, some visually impaired students may sometimes resist disclosing the nature of their sight loss at least in some situations. It is important to be sensitive to this and to issues of confidentiality.

For higher education staff, medical definitions can be surprisingly unimportant since they sometimes do not provide quick or relevant answers to learning-related questions. What does a diagnosis of 3/60 sight loss actually mean when it comes to maximizing access to learning materials? Even condition-specific information such as 'tunnel vision' may be of somewhat limited use since the degree, stability and severity of the student's eye condition as it relates to accessing the chosen curriculum is a far greater issue. In other words, working with the student to assess his or her degree and type of functional vision in study-related settings is usually the initial issue. How then can the student's performance and attainment be maximized in lectures, tutorials, online learning, the lab, on work placements and in fieldwork? What teaching and learning strategies need to be brought in to support the student's independent working?

Accessible teaching and learning strategies

Sight loss is 'one of the commonest causes of disability in the UK' (RNIB, 1997). And although it is a relatively low incidence disability within higher education, numbers of visually impaired students are increasing year by year. Representation currently stands at several thousand.

Because of relatively low incidence, however, it is inevitable that there will be many occasions where teaching and support staff encounter a visually impaired student for the first time. When this occurs, a balance needs to be struck between awareness of good practice which covers most visually impaired students as a group (such as the necessary quality of print material as defined by good practice guidelines such as RNIB's *See it Right*) and response to the learning and support needs of the individual student (such as the size of print provided, or the necessity to use non-visual methods entirely). In addition, when staff have limited prior experience in working with visually impaired students, an awareness of individual differences also becomes critical. The difference may be as great as one student studying completely by non-sighted methods, combining tape, personal readers, and screen-reading software for speech and/or Braille access to the PC; while another student is studying entirely by means of large print, enlarged text on screen and hand-held low vision aids in lectures. Difference could, though, occur just as easily between two partially sighted students, one with no central vision and one with no peripheral vision (that is, with tunnel vision). Large print is likely to assist the former student but may not suit the latter.

Further, visually impaired students as an overall group often combine sighted and non-sighted study methods, using residual sight when possible and non-sighted methods as back-up. The right combination requires initial specialist assessment, the balancing of low-tech and high-tech solutions, and the ongoing commitment by staff to enable the student to maximize use of a range of study methods while on-course. The summary boxes provided are designed to offer staff initial checklists when working with visually impaired students to offer appropriate adaptations. An overall guiding principle, though, is the offering of equal access to materials normally provided in standard print. Equal access may require transcription, preparation time and production cost. Wider checklists for providing accessible information are provided by the RNIB (2001).

Guidelines for adapting teaching strategy and the learning environment for visually impaired students

- Agree adaptations with the student and, in small group situations such as tutorials, with the group itself: for example, initial consistency in seating location to assist a blind student to recognize group members' voices, group members initially agreeing to give their first name before speaking.
- Provide material in advance of a lecture or tutorial in the student's preferred format, such as OHP slides or tutorial discussion notes in print, large print, disk or Braille.
- Take account of lighting and the possibility of glare: for example, tutors not sitting with a source of light directly behind them or reducing glare by closing blinds.
- Encourage visually impaired students to use 'paper/pen' substitutes such as tape recorders or laptops during lectures.
- Give thought to verbal and non-verbal communication, trying to eliminate background noise, speaking clearly, and avoiding inacces-

sible gestures such as a nod of the head and expressions such as 'it's over there'.

- Allow visually impaired students additional time, if required, for assignments and examinations/assessments.
- Allow equal access to visual materials such as video, for example, by also providing a transcript or loaning the video to the student in advance.
- Assist students by prioritizing texts in a booklist if visual impairment limits the research time that the student can reasonably give to the task.

Learning and information can be made accessible to visually impaired students in many different ways. Disk, tape, large print, clear print design, Braille, e-text, accessible Web sites, and tactile diagrams account for almost all appropriate adaptations. Some formats such as Braille or tape need forward planning. Though sometimes not essential, it is good practice to have all learning materials available in advance in all study media, but there needs to be scope for a prompt response to individual student needs. For instance, curriculum materials might be made available as computer text for easy sending to visually impaired students on disk, by e-mail or for sending to a local society for the blind which could offer Brailling facilities. If the higher education establishment does not provide some formatting options centrally or departmentally (such as Brailling, raised diagram copying or taping), does the institution have a network of connections with third parties who will offer a set turn-round time? Ideally, this type of organizational cooperation is built in to forward planning with visually impaired students, so that they can obtain learning materials in their preferred format either before other students or at the same time as them. The box provides some guidelines for three of the commonest types of curriculum adaptation.

Guidelines for providing accessible information to visually impaired students

Print and images

- The majority of visually impaired students want to read print material if it is made accessible for them.

- Use 14 point large print as a minimum general size for visually impaired students, but if possible ask the student what an optimum size will be (usually 16 to 22 point).
- Use bold or semi–bold type weight rather than light or roman.
- Avoid highly stylized typefaces and typestyles such as ornamental or display faces, and omit italics, use of unnecessary capitals, and underlining.
- Use the same amount of space between each word, and avoid aligning text to the right or centred text (that is, use left alignment only).
- If using contrasts between the text and background, contrast dark against light, and also be aware of students' individual contrast needs.
- Avoid text that runs round images if the image requires lines of text to begin in different places down a ragged edge against it.
- Avoid overlaying text on images or images on images.
- If using large print, it can generally be produced on desktop PCs using word processing software.

E-text

- Communicating by e-mail with visually impaired students on campus may often be the fastest, most convenient solution for staff and students.
- Partially sighted students may be accessing the information by using large screens or text enlargement packages, so the document needs clear, simple design.
- Blind students may be accessing the e-text by using a screen-reader reading the screen with speech or Braille output.
- Ensure there is a text equivalent for information other than straight text: graphics, images and highlights.
- Convert tables to text or present them as spreadsheets and send as Excel files: ask the student which he or she would prefer.
- Use filenames that will mean something for the student, and consider how best to phrase the subject line of the e-mail.
- Try to label floppy disks being sent in large print or Braille; the RNIB provides simple Braille dymo labelling guns to help staff apply labels to wallets or cases easily (dymo labels should not be applied to the CDs themselves).

Tape

- External organizations will tend to produce entire texts on tape, and the student may also recruit volunteer readers paid for from Disabled Students' Allowance.
- Advise external organizations whether an entire text is absolutely required, or whether selected portions such as chapters will suffice.
- Any staff and student volunteers reading on to tape on-site should take account of good practice guides such as the checklist for tape production provided by COTIS, the UK organization for ensuring the quality of tape productions.
- Similarly, staff and student volunteers should make use of technology such as four-track recorders and external tone-indexing units available from the RNIB: these should ensure that recordings made by staff are easy to listen to.
- Check the acoustics and that the machine and microphone are working properly.
- Start the tape by giving name of reader, date of recording, contents, what each side contains, which tones start each section, and how long the tape and recording are.
- Label cassette cases in large print and/or Braille.

Learning is a collaboration between staff and the student, and to a large extent visually impaired students need to work out how best to proceed with higher education. Some of this can be assessed, particularly when it is to involve choice of access technology and choice of basic methods such as using tape, Braille, or large print. Whether there is a need to utilize sighted readers is another very basic issue. However, some study issues may not be as clear-cut as these, and some may emerge as the course progresses.

How to make notes efficiently in lectures can be one such issue. Visually impaired students may request that they use non-visual note-taking methods, but may also seek to work out an agreed strategy with lecturers for accessing boardwork and OHP material. To begin with, some experimentation may be necessary before the best solution is found. Generally, taping lectures is best as a back-up method only, since each hour of recording can require several hours of transcription. Some students use dictaphones, others use silent Braille and laptop devices in class. Also, unless a recording is digital and allows levels of navigation, listening to material is a 'linear' process and can therefore become very passive. Visually impaired students using tape for any significant period of time are therefore advised to use a twin deck or similar system to record key phrases or ideas on to a second tape. Use of headphones and varying the speed of play can also improve concentration and keep listening as active a task as possible.

Another issue that can arise is the necessity to sometimes access very visual curricular material: maps, diagrams, graphs or photographs. Sometimes the material can be described to the student verbally at length, perhaps initially onto tape with the lecturer and student working together. An enlarged and clearer version can also be considered. However, blind students may require tactile diagrams, and this may incur a cost. Tactile diagrams can be made manually and thermoformed (vacuum-formed), Braille embossed, or designed on computer and printed out in tactile form.

The relationship that is struck between visually impaired students and teaching staff is critical at a number of levels. If an understanding is reached about provision of accessible material and similar inclusion issues, the student should be able to gain equal access to the learning process along with sighted peers. Students' motivation will also improve, and they will feel they are being given a fair chance. The two case studies below are recent verbatim transcripts from two visually impaired university students, both answering a question to do with their perceptions of lecturers' attitudes towards them.

Case study 1: Guy

All lecturers have been really good. I mean, they let me get on with it and don't try and hold my hand. Treat me as an equal. I think at first they could have been a little apprehensive about what I can do. 'What can he see, how are we going to. ...' I think the learning support coordinator helped to prepare the ground enough. I've not once been aware of any kind of patronizing attitude or frustrated attitude or negative attitude towards me.

Case Study 2: Sarah

Lecturers this semester have been excellent actually. There has been no hassle at all. A couple at the beginning of the semester last year came into the psychology lecture, and one of them switched off the tape recorder at the front - after me already asking them. But I went up and said something to them and it got sorted out, kind of thing. They didn't

> really appreciate the lectures being taped but they had the situation explained, which I thought I'd already done ... but it was explained a second time. I think there has been trouble in the past with lecturers but I think it was smoothed over by the time I got here which is good.

Overall, staff should never underestimate the impact of visual impairment on learning. Sometimes there is the assumption that a student will study and succeed largely without stress if the Disabled Students' Allowance and reader support are accessed, and if appropriate teaching strategies are employed. However, staff still need to recognize the issue of time. It is very likely that a visually impaired student will still need more time to study, even if the right level of support is offered. Tasks involving access technology are likely to take longer if comparisons are made with sighted students. The students need to manage their time very effectively. Students with a visual impairment also have additional responsibilities that sighted students need not bother with. Sighted readers and any other assistance organized through Disabled Students' Allowance have to be worked with in constructive ways. This involves meetings, planning, ensuring others' assistance is helpful, and the maintenance of a supportive network.

The impact of access technology

In 2001, the Technology for Disabilities Information Service (TechDis) was formed by JISC. Based in York at the Institute for Learning and Teaching, it subsumed DISinHE and provides an information service to the further and higher education sector. This service aims to enhance access to learning for students and staff with disabilities, and to promote innovative practice in access technology. More specific to visual impairment, the RNIB's Technology in Learning and Employment (TiLE) department has been established to work strategically with other organizations to make technology increasingly accessible to, among other groups, visually impaired students. Although substantial progress has been made in making technology accessible to students, significant challenges remain. Virtual learning environments, the software that controls the presentation of learning resources, is one such challenge at the time of writing. Further work with the authors of learning modules will assist in developing good practice for accessible multimedia materials.

RNIB TiLE produces a number of accessible technology factsheets (http://www.rnib.org.uk/technology/factsheets/factsheets.htm) designed for visually impaired students and their higher education staff. Each factsheet gives advice on buying the equipment, types of technology available with specifications on the options, and supplier information. Some are also broad enough to cover basic procedures required of students within higher education. For instance, the factsheet about note taking covers Braille and speech note takers, PC type notebooks, cassette recorders, and digital recorders. The factsheet describing access to the Internet assists students with questions such as choosing an Internet Service Provider, Web page accessibility, the equipment required and online sources of information.

Accessing Technology (Cain, 2001) is an RNIB publication that includes information about using technology to support the learning and employment opportunities for visually impaired users. This resource is valuable for any staff working with visually impaired students. It provides information about available technology, case studies to show how it is used practically, and articles that highlight specific issues around the use of technology.

Often, all the technology required by a visually impaired student for higher education can be obtained by means of the Disabled Students' Allowance. This does require, however, an expert assessment of study and technology needs, with the report usually going to the student's local education authority. An assessment pre-entry is ideal but is not a requirement. Any such assessment should enable the student to identify individual study and learning support needs, identify technology needs and how they can be matched to products and training, and gain access to funding. As higher education progresses, a student's technology needs may well change. This will be because of new course subject requirements, advances in standard technology, and fluctuations or deterioration in the student's degree of useful sight.

At the level of the higher education establishment, there is increasing investment in access technology for visually impaired students. Often this involves the purchase of site licences from suppliers for multiple user options across several campuses. In terms of actual location of this technology, visually impaired students tend to report a preference for unobtrusive and inclusive access. PCs with appropriate software installed can be located in generic clusters in libraries and study centres rather than in discrete locations. The latter option may marginalize visually impaired students' study and social time in relation to sighted peers. It is also important that the establishment's computer services staff are given appropriate training to support visually impaired students, who are increasingly using highly sophisticated and specialized technology. Telephone support from specialist hardware and software suppliers, though useful, is often insufficient to enable full use of the products.

Accessible technology case study: RNIB TiLE and the University of Glasgow Department of Psychology

Making SPSS accessible for visually impaired students

Until recently, blind students were unable to access the Statistical Package for the Social Sciences (SPSS) independently. They could not analyse research data from their own projects, since SPSS features, such as arrow buttons for variable selection, were inaccessible for blind users. They were therefore required to make use of staff support and student assistance, imposing considerable barriers to independent learning. The debate in *Nature* (Dimigen, Roy and Burton, 1999; Earl and Leventhal, 1999; Orme, Dimigen and Roy, 1999) reveals how SPSS accessibility questions such as these were tackled by research staff in the United Kingdom and United States at different stages. Much of the software development work occurred off campus at the RNIB, while the trialling of potential solutions occurred at the university with active cooperation from blind students and recent graduates.

It is important for staff and visually impaired students to realize that SPSS can be used with the JAWS screen reader, which has been configured to relay all the necessary SPSS information such as data entry grids and dialogue boxes to the blind computer user. Other similarly complex applications used by students may or may not provide such effective access, and some investigation will have to be done to establish the usability of any software that a student wishes or needs to use.

The RNIB TiLE is now working with the developers of SPSS in the United States to ensure that future versions of SPSS provide enhanced accessibility for users with visual impairments and other disabilities.

Visually impaired students use a variety of different access technology options to read the computer screen, and the choice of solution needs to be considered carefully, preferably in the light of information provided by an expert who knows about both access technology and the higher education sector. Screen magnification programs are commonly used by students, but if the student has too little useful vision to use the computer screen effectively with magnification alone, then speech output can be added in support. If magnification does not meet the student's needs, even with the addition of supporting speech output, a screen reading program is required. This converts information taken from the computer screen to speech output, and optionally also to an electronic Braille display (sometimes mistakenly called a Braille keyboard). The Braille display manipulates small pins within eight-pin Braille 'cells' which selectively pop up to represent Braille characters. Braille uses only six dots per character, and the two extra pins per cell on the display are used to represent the position of the cursor, and other information that cannot be represented in the standard Braille code.

Higher education staff, however, need to be aware that access technology is only one part of the support jigsaw in relation to visually impaired students. Low-tech solutions are also important. Coloured non-glare plastic wallets for holding paper and an adjustable lectern for comfortable writing are just two examples of possible low-tech solutions. In fact, supporting visually impaired students requires a much wider system of inclusion which has as one of its core features the prioritizing of access technology and the resourcing of it, perhaps from capital budgets.

Psychological effects of visual impairment

The psychological dimension can apply both to visually impaired students and to staff encountering students for the first time. Society can make sharp distinctions, such as between blindness and sight. The question of partial sight remains, and people with any one of the vast range of conditions that cause partial sight may often have been subjected to misunderstanding and outright prejudice. This also applies to blindness, but Sacks (1996) outlines the further, compounding barrier of others' complete lack of understanding and awareness in relation to partial sight. She notes from her experience that sometimes people are relieved when they are registered as blind rather than partially sighted, because they feel that others will offer them greater understanding; at least blindness is a known concept. For a partially sighted student, the fully sighted world's expectation may well have been: if you can see this, you must be able to see that as well. The fully sighted world may accuse partially sighted people of 'faking it'.

Conrod and Overbury (1998) discuss some of the problematic issues partial sight can give rise to, whether it is acquired or congenital: 'Persons with low vision do not appear to be disabled and thus are caught in a dilemma: they either make excuses for awkward or incompetent behaviour or attempt to conceal the fact that they have low vision. In both cases, the result is often further isolation, inactivity and withdrawal.' Many visually impaired students have learnt how to communicate their disability well, but may still be reluctant at times to do so. Self-disclosure is a skill that needs to be taken on board and practised in a variety of situations.

The literature documents society's negative attitudes towards visually impaired people. There is also evidence, though, that visually impaired students will often give sighted students and lecturers every opportunity to overcome any ignorance, stereotyping or prejudice! A number of strategies can be employed such as humour, putting sighted people at ease, assertiveness, and clear disclosure of degree of sight loss. The evidence from students is that most staff are very willing to assist when they know about students' sight loss, but without knowing initially how best to help. Beyond the level of a student guiding members of staff in how best to assist with materials, the disability lobby and the Quality Assurance Agency for Higher Education have documented the clear need for disability equality staff training. There is also a need, though, for any such training to include input on the personal and educational impact of visual impairment. This can offer useful support to staff who may experience anxiety and apprehension when faced with the unfamiliarity of teaching a visually impaired student.

Most of the visually impaired students interviewed in a recent research exercise (Roy, 2001) felt positive about sight loss. However, some did go into detail about the personal and social challenges and barriers they had been required to overcome. Evidence suggested that those growing up with full sight and only subsequently experiencing sight loss, perhaps in late teenage years, had experienced considerable personal trauma related to the loss. This should not, though, be associated too much with the concept of 'bereavement'. Adaptation after sudden sight loss has more to do with re-adjustment, learning to be independent again and, at a deeper level, re-evaluating who one is as a person. At the same time, blind students with long-term loss of sight may experience issues created by new challenges. They may sometimes feel that others' expectations require them to maintain the appearance of being successful.

For students who participated in this research, current success in higher education was part of the process of moving on, succeeding in a competitive environment, and showing friends and family what was achievable. This whole dimension of coming to terms with visual impairment, moving through negative towards positive stages of adjustment, was much less of an issue, understandably, in students whose sight loss was lifelong and stable. This was particularly the case if students had never experienced any useful sight. For partially sighted students whose sight loss has been stable, there is still the realization that others may misperceive them, and that some level of independence is denied to them (such as driving). Again, the individual differences are important for higher education staff to take into account. Two very different examples follow.

Case study: Faye discussing academic staff attitudes

You learn very, very quickly that you ask and you don't get. You have to plead or do it yourself most of the time. There's always somebody somewhere who'll be willing to help you. You just need to find them! They [lecturers] don't want to approach you for fear of embarrassing you or patronizing you probably, whereas you've been drowning for months at the time.

[Visual impairment] has created a hell of a lot of barriers. Created people's perceptions of you before they know you. If you bump into something, people will think you're drunk or something. And in myself as well.

Case study: Kirsty discussing her aspirations and transition from her undergraduate degree

At the moment I'm making plans for this. I'm going to do some work experience at a special school and then in a children and family centre. And then in two mainstream schools. These are all just plans at the moment. I've also approached the postgraduate educational psychology tutor already, and he's told me the kind of experience I should get. We have talked about ways round the course and round the actual job.

And will it be you shaping the future, or will it be other people and situations out of your control?

Well, I'm hoping it will be me, because I've heard reports from some blind people that they have tried to get into educational psychology and had a negative reaction. But I had it all planned out and how my

answers would be before I approached the tutor, and every time he
came up with a problem, I had a possible solution, so hopefully I'll get
round these situations. And they will be in my control.

Practical classes

Sometimes higher education staff are particularly concerned about visually
impaired students involved in practical elements within courses. Staff can be
particularly concerned about health and safety issues in subjects such as
biological sciences, medicine and subjects allied to medicine. Visually
impaired students study in all these fields (though representation has been
fairly low), and it is likely that most specific access issues have already been
addressed and resolved by one or more higher education institutions. Some
strategies and preparation issues can be detailed here but accessing this type
of curriculum is covered more fully by Owen Hutchinson, Atkinson and
Orpwood (1998).

Visually impaired students should be given adequate preparation time,
and this will involve prior background reading and detailed handouts. The
nature of any equipment to be used in lab work should be explained in
detail. The lab should be laid out carefully and in an ordered way, with
particular attention being given to colour contrasts and suitable ambient
lighting. The student could be involved in the setting-up stage if staff
believe this will aid his or her understanding. Thereafter, a number of
enhanced teaching and health and safety strategies should come into play.
The student should be encouraged to be methodical, with particular attention to tidiness. All students involved in any lab work, including the visually
impaired student, must be encouraged to relocate all equipment in its identified place. Staff should increase their explanation of techniques during
demonstrations, and allow the student any desirable additional practice
time. This can be considered almost as a standard adaptation to course
delivery when good practice and good health and safety principles are
being adhered to.

Procedures or skills demonstrated in their entirety should then be broken
down into their constituent parts, so that each can be explained, demonstrated and worked through. Partially sighted students should be encouraged to position themselves so that they use useful residual sight to
maximum benefit. Blind students should, where appropriate, be encouraged
to feel different stages in a demonstration. Even just feeling the location of

different pieces of equipment may help the student understand the processes involved. Health and safety requirements may dictate that a student uses touch to support any residual vision when it comes to checking the location of equipment and any potential hazards. Further, visually impaired students sometimes use lab assistants paid for through Disabled Students' Allowance. Requirements may also have to be audited and adapted to satisfy any additional needs. Hopefully these pointers are helpful, but they are by no means comprehensive. More detailed guidelines should be obtained from the references and further reading detailed at the end of this chapter.

Overview and conclusion

This chapter has outlined some of the main inclusive learning issues that staff need to take account of when working with visually impaired students. It has also provided some detail on individual differences between students. Differences exist within a range of study strategies and access technology options. The range as a whole will serve to maximize students' equal access to learning. All the strategies and options have an impact on, and implications for, staff seeking to offer a genuinely equal opportunity.

Some of the individual and psychological issues to do with disclosure of sight loss and adjustment have also been explored. Staff need to set aside any stereotyped views about visual impairment and its implications for studying. Presenting the curriculum creatively and applying innovation will allow staff to break down the barriers to learning faced by visually impaired students. Resources and expertise within and beyond the higher education sector exist to assist staff with the curriculum-related challenges that may sometimes arise.

References

Cain, S (2001) *Accessing Technology*, RNIB, London

Conrod, B E and Overbury, O (1998) The effectiveness of perceptual training and psychosocial counselling in adjustment to the loss of vision, *Journal of Visual Impairment and Blindness*, **92** (7), pp 464–82

Dimigen, G, Roy, A W N and Burton, A M (1999) Information technology and visual impairment: new developments, *Nature*, **397** (6720), Software Reviews [online] 18 February

Earl, C L and Leventhal, J D (1999) An evaluation of the accessibility of the SPSS 8.0 statistical package with a screen reader, *Nature*, **397** (6720), Software Reviews [online] 18 February

Orme, R, Dimigen, G and Roy, A W N (1999) A screen reader solution for accessing SPSS 9.0 without sight, *Nature*, **401** (6755), Software Reviews [online] 21 October

Owen Hutchinson, J, Atkinson, K and Orpwood, J (1998) *Breaking Down Barriers: Access to further and higher education for visually impaired students*, Stanley Thornes, Cheltenham

Richardson, J T E and Roy, A W N (2002) The representation and attainment of students with a visual impairment in higher education, *British Journal of Visual Impairment*, **20** (1), pp 37–48

Roy, A W N (2001) *Student Perspectives: Discussions with visually impaired students on the effects of serious sight loss on themselves, their families and friends*, RNIB, London

Royal National Institute for the Blind (RNIB) (1997) *Blindness: The facts*, RNIB, London

RNIB (2001) *See it Right*, RNIB, London

Sacks, S Z (1996) Psychological and social implications of low vision, in *Foundations of Low Vision: Clinical and functional perspectives*, ed A L Corn and A J Koenig, American Foundation for the Blind, New York

Scottish Higher Education Funding Council (SHEFC) (2000) Teachability: Creating an Accessible Curriculum for Students with Disabilities, SHEFC, Glasgow.

Simkiss, P, Garner, S and Dryden, G (1998) *What Next? The experience of transition*, RNIB, London

Further reading

McCandlish, C (2000) *Lifelong Learning: Improving opportunities for visually impaired older adults*, *RNIB*, London

RNIB (2001) *Shaping the Future: The educational experiences of blind and partially sighted young people aged 16 to 25*, RNIB, London

Useful contact addresses

The Association of Blind and Partially Sighted Teachers and Students (ABAPSTAS) provides a discussion forum, runs courses and exhibitions of equipment and publishes a quarterly magazine in print, tape and Braille.
ABAPSTAS, BM Box 6727, London WC1N 3XX
Tel: 01484 517954
Web site: www.abapstas.freeservers.com

The British Computer Association of the Blind (BCAB) is a self-help group of visually impaired computer users and professionals.
BCAB, BM Box 950, London WC1N 3XX
Tel: 02476 369533
e-mail: info@bcab.org.uk
Web site: www.bcab.org.uk

COTIS is an organization which seeks to improve tape recording and presentation standards. Its checklist can assist staff to check quality of internal tape production and that of third parties.
COTIS Secretary, Project Office, 67 High Street, Tarporley, Cheshire CW6 0DP
Tel: 01829 732115

Staff and visually impaired students requiring advice and support with mobility training should make contact with a Mobility Officer. Local social services offices, education authority visual impairment teams and liaison officers at the Guide Dogs for the Blind Association may all be able to help.
Guide Dogs for the Blind Association (GDBA),
Hillfields, Burghfield, Reading, Berkshire RG7 3YG
Tel: 0118 9835555
Web site: www.gdba.org.uk

The National Centre for Tactile Diagrams offers an archive of educational diagrams, design and production expertise and consultancy.
Dr Sarah Morley, Director
National Centre for Tactile Diagrams
University of Hertfordshire, Hatfield, Herts AL10 9AB
Tel: 01707 285285
Web site: www.nctd.org.uk

The Royal National Institute for the Blind (RNIB) employs a regionally-based network of Post-Sixteen Education Officers who can assist staff and visually impaired students. Support includes advice on course options, guidance, staff development and training, input on teaching and learning strategies, and inclusion auditing. The RNIB's Technology Officers can support students and staff in choice of and training with access technology.

RNIB Education and Employment Division

105 Judd Street, London WC1H 9NE

Helpline tel: 0845 766 9999

e-mail: helpline@rnib.org.uk

Web site: www.rnib.org.uk

Student Web site: www.rnib.org.uk/student

6

Able student, disabled person: access to courses in higher education by students with physical disabilities

Alan V Jones and Christopher Hopkins

Introduction

This chapter will address the general problems students with physical disabilities experience when applying to, and studying in, higher education. Some case studies will be used to emphasize the principles being considered.

The nature of access

It is our contention, and that of many others, that true access into higher education by students with disabilities means a right to enter all appropriate courses. These include those involving the practical sciences, technology, medicine, teaching, engineering and sports science, providing the students have the academic qualifications and abilities to do so. Disabled people should not be restricted, as some school career advisers recommend, to the more 'book' based courses if the student has the academic ability, common sense, genuine desire and motivation to do the appropriate courses. This chapter focuses upon students with physical disabilities and their access to suitable courses.

'Access' here means finding the most appropriate place and course in which to study, so maximizing the student's abilities to their limit. This process might mean a time of searching for such suitable university courses on the part of the prospective student with a physical disability, in order to find places that have supportive atmospheres and suitably adapted facilities. It also requires students to have sought suitable advice related to their own abilities and limitations for tackling such courses. Access clearly does not mean lowering of academic standards. Standards are not going to be lowered in the world of work, so why should they in higher education?

Admissions tutors must 'tune in' to the needs of some students whose situation they may never have encountered before. In this chapter, the authors have assumed that each higher education institution (HEI) has a specific service/department responsible for providing disability advice to current and prospective students, and perhaps to disabled members of staff as well. Whatever provision they do make for disabled people, each HEI must periodically produce a Disability Statement that sets out the provision made for disabled people. In our experience most professionals feel there needs to be a realistic transparency of course content and accessibility to facilities in prospectuses in higher education. Obviously, some HEIs are much stronger than others in the provision they make.

The National Bureau for Students with Disabilities (Skill) is a priceless resource for both students and those who work with them, and produces regular updated information, runs courses and conferences, and is setting up an Internet discussion list for disabled students (see 'Useful contacts').

Are courses open to all or are there limitations?

It may be argued that each subject area has its own culture and set of academic expectations, which a student must appreciate. Students with physical disabilities will also have to match any practical work expected during the course with their own strengths and limitations.

The theoretical concepts involved in most subjects can be open to any student with the ability to work with abstract ideas. These can be very stimulating but the question arises, particularly in the science and engineering areas, 'Can the practical work be undertaken by students with physical disabilities?' Departments must ask if there is a need to do all the practical work to become, for example, a professional chemist; if any disabilities should automatically bar a person from doing a course; whether or not facilities are suitable. These issues must be addressed before claims can be made of an 'open access' policy in their prospectus.

Readers (if working in a university) might need to stop and think at this stage what limitations they or particular departments in their institutions would put on, for example, a 'wheelchair user' or 'visually impaired' student applying to do for example chemistry, medicine or any of the engineering subjects. Are there areas of these subjects that might have to be tackled in a 'theoretical' way rather than in a 'practical hands on' manner? Does this make the eventual graduate any less of a professional? Clearly there are some limitations here, and it would be unwise for a person with hand/eye coordination problems to become a surgeon. In reality of course, the person probably already realizes that, and in any case entry into other areas of, in this case, medicine should not be judged on the basis of this extreme scenario.

- Could a wheelchair user do environmental science or chemical engineering?
- Would a person requiring to use a wheelchair most of the time be acceptable as a trainee teacher?
- Can a person with a physical disability study sports science?
- Would a social studies degree course be accessible and useful to a housebound person?
- Are there possibilities of some distance learning modules in some of the degree programmes to help alleviate daily travel? Are there video link-ups available via the 'net' for any course modules of individual lectures?

Ten years ago the answer to all these questions would have been 'no'. But what about now in the reader's own university? The authors know of degree programmes that put some lectures on the Web. Is this too innovative, or is it just too much of a hassle?

Some degree courses are also vetted and validated by professional organizations such as the GMC for medicine, 'the Institutions' for the various branches of engineering, and the British Psychological Society for psychology. University departments will frequently argue that their hands are tied by the requirements laid down by an external organization that will only accept the awarding of the qualification under certain restrictive conditions.

It is hoped that such problems will be addressed in a project at Loughborough University for prospective engineers (Hopkins, work in progress).

National school curriculum/education acts/Disability Discrimination Act: their effects upon admission to higher education

Since 1989 the National Curriculum in England and Wales has sought to ensure that a full, balanced curriculum is available to all who can benefit from it. It has included, for the first time, pupils with special needs who had previously had no entitlement to a balanced education. The Education Act incorporating 'Curriculum 2000' has strengthened these entitlements. In our view, these open up much greater educational opportunities and real prospects of inclusion for any prospective university students.

In the past, if pupils lost a lot of schooling because of time in hospital, they were often placed in special schools where their educational potential may not have been fully developed. (We are not being critical of special schools per se here, but rather suggesting that misplacements may have been made.) Since 1989 and into the 21st century, the move towards integration and inclusion of all suitable pupils into 'mainstream' schools and the restructuring of specially designated schools have been significant. Now it can be argued that the full curriculum is available to any pupil able to benefit from it. If the school curriculum up to the age of 16 has been opened up to all pupils, there should be more pupils with disabilities and learning difficulties entering courses at 16+ (A or AS level, HTEC, NVQ, GNVQ, colleges of further education etc). The design of modular school A and AS syllabuses also builds in a potential for greater flexibility than previously experienced. Certainly there has been a growth in vocational education and post-16 courses available to many pupils/students who had previously not been considered, or who had lost educational opportunities due to lack of schooling in their early years. Chris Hopkins, one of the authors, is an example of this. He missed a lot of study time in school due to hospitalization and so on, but later in life was given various opportunities, and eventually completed a Master's Degree at Leeds University.

Many universities have been innovative in opening up their courses by providing a more flexible approach to studies, and the Open University (OU, 1991) is a good example of this. But the question remains as to whether or not the more conventional universities are making their courses more 'disabled friendly'. Do they see a need to do so, to enable students with physical disabilities to reach their goal of a degree, or do they see such effort as an unnecessary expense? Those in the latter camp may interpret building modifications and adaptations to accommodation as too great a gamble to take in case 'the students leave and so affect drop-out rates'. This may then affect their national rating, as student numbers and funding are often judged in part by the drop-out rates. Conversely some institutions have seen making provision as a means of boosting their numbers of committed students, by catering for what others universities fail to recognize.

Science and engineering for students with physical disabilities

There is a national (and international) lack of science and engineering students, and a question arises whether institutions are preventing some prospective students from even considering entering these subject areas because of hidden agendas and wrong messages too early in the education process. 'Oh, *you* can't do science/technology as a career, you are disabled, you had better stick to the IT and history courses', advised one, not atypical, career adviser.

Can you be a theoretical mathematician, scientist or engineer and only do limited practical work? I hope so, as we might miss another Stephen Hawking. We wonder if he would be accepted in your university if he applied now? It says in the introduction of *Skill into Science and Engineering* (Skill, 1997), 'Many disabled people have successfully studied science and engineering at undergraduate and post graduate levels and are now pursuing rewarding careers. Modern technology, flexibility and creative approach have opened doors, which previously appeared to be locked shut.'

Another very big consideration is admission into professional organizations, and their influence and control over entry to courses. Most, if not all, the professional bodies (such as those in medicine, science and engineering) have 'equal opportunities' policies for access to the professions by disabled people.

In Chapter 4 of *Able Scientist/Technologist, Disabled Person* (Hopkins and Jones, 2000), the President of the Institution of Electrical Engineers says:

> It is fair to say that many of the developments which members have been working on, particularly in communication, computing, electronics and control systems, will actually make it easier for a disabled person, whatever the disability, to follow their chosen education and career path. It is estimated that we have a potential shortfall of 50,000 specialists in these areas and there

is no reason why a person with a disability cannot carve out a career. Consider also the manufacturing industry where computer aided design and production now assists everyone whether they have a disability or not … at the moment engineering is not attracting enough talented people.

The Disability Discrimination Act (DDA) and its high ideals, if it is going to succeed to influence society, require disabled people to be in the mainstream workplace. If there are no students with physical disabilities in higher education, there will be a layer of management without disability awareness in industry and commerce. So it behoves the universities to think seriously about providing access to students with disabilities and not operate 'tokenism'. Would the current government cabinet minister, David Blunkett, have been accepted on your course, along with his guide dog? Would you have allowed him to do a 'practical subject'?

Admission procedure

Declaration of disability

One basic strategy for admission tutors noting a declaration by a suitably qualified student of a physical disability on his or her application form is to arrange a visit. If a disabled person is accepted, there should be no reason why an HEI is not able to provide all the academic and non-academic related support he or she requires. It is essential that students check out for themselves access to all the facilities, and it is also essential that the university has a well-documented policy and procedure, as accepting a disabled student means catering for *all* their needs. The university disability officer should know all the requirements and agencies to contact for help.

If a student is accepted on paper qualifications alone, and does not declare his or her physical disability (for whatever reason: for example, fear of rejection on the course), the university is not automatically responsible for supplying all his or her requirements. But if a declaration has been made on the forms and has been missed by the admission tutor, the university is responsible for providing suitable accessible facilities. One case particularly comes to mind, during that hectic period of 'Clearing' where an inexperienced admissions tutor accepted a student and missed the declaration on the form of his disability and requirements. On the student's arrival it became apparent that he was a wheelchair user, and most of the lectures for the course were on floors inaccessible to him. A 'stair crawler' had to be installed hastily, and the Dean was not pleased with the additional expense.

Accessibility is particularly important in the subjects involving practical workshops and laboratories.

Each university must now have a person responsible for disabled students, and this person usually gets involved with interviews and open days if a declaration is made on the application form. But this takes time, effort and hence money. If this procedure is followed, in time we may see the numbers of disabled students entering HE rise from the current value of approximately 3–4 per cent.

Attitudes of admission tutors

Disabled people who are considering embarking on a higher education course nowadays can find out about the places that are of interest to them by either requesting a copy of a Disability Statement or viewing it on the institution's Web pages. Again, members of staff at an HEI who may well have taken on a role for disability matters as well as retaining their main post are advised to turn to the Internet for some support. The Joint Information System Committee (JISC) discussion list 'dis-forum' is especially for disability coordinators and advisers within HE and FE. JISC also hosts another discussion list concerned with disabled people and technology called 'dis-tech' (for contact details of JISC see 'Useful contacts').

For the book *Able Scientist/Technologist, Disabled Person* (Hopkins and Jones, 2000) a number of admission tutors for science, engineering and medical courses were contacted in a wide range of universities and colleges, and their responses make interesting reading. It is clear from those responses that proactive procedures have been adopted by most departments in universities to open up opportunities for disabled students. Here is an edited version of one encounter told to us by an admission tutor.

'Can I please come to visit your department prior to making an application?' asked a prospective student. The exchange of correspondence proved extremely fruitful. The tutor and mature student Robert arranged to meet prior to an open day, and the tutor was a little surprised and somewhat embarrassed to find that Robert was a wheelchair user with very limited mobility, something that he had not clearly understood when reading the letter Robert wrote.

Robert relieved the tension obvious in the tutor's face by saying, 'It's OK, my brain still functions, although sometimes my hands and mouth take some time to catch up,' and the two started their conversation in a much easier atmosphere. Robert explained his point of view that if you are too explicit about your disability, many university departments will not even interview you. It was obvious that there was no impairment in this student's thinking, although it took a little time for the interviewer to fully understand the occasional word. When he was in doubt, a written word or a rephrasing of the sentence did the trick. Initially the tutor was a little embarrassed as the department did not get many applications from disabled students, but he was put at his ease when Robert told a joke about how someone had misinterpreted some of his words with amusing results.

This edited conversation of a tutor with Robert was prior to the latter applying for a place on a science course.

Q: How difficult has it been for you to study for your A levels in school?

A: The school advised me at the age of 14 to do a single science GCSE, which limited my A level choices. My loss of schooling in primary school and the early part of my secondary school also meant that I lacked suitable qualifications at the age of 16. They seemed inflexible about allowing me to stay with other, younger groups of pupils until I caught up. I left school with a desire to learn more, so I took a part-time college course to upgrade my meagre qualifications. This took some time as I had to get a job to get money to live. I was 25 before I was satisfied with my pre-university qualifications at GCSE and A level.

Q: Were you born with a disability or did you become disabled? Does this make a difference?

A: I was born with spina bifida and have known no other lifestyle, so what you know as a disability has been normal for me, though this is not to say that I didn't go through some difficult periods during my teens. Generally I get on and try to overcome the barriers other non-disabled people put up, like access to buildings, stairs, libraries, transport, rush hour meal times in cafés and so on.

     Others who have become disabled, say after an accident, sometimes find difficulty in adapting to these barriers, and some even opt out of the challenge, so they need encouragement to break out of this mindset and restructure their lives to give them maximum personal and professional satisfaction. Some are initially angry and bitter, and need help during this time of adjustment. I have helped one or two through this trauma in the past.

Q: Have you visited any other university departments?

A: Some thought I would be suitable for an HND because I had lost so much schooling, and some would not even consider me, although I have better entry qualifications than their average student. I was put off by some tutors because of their negative attitude and the problems they could see for themselves by accepting me. After preliminary visits at the open days at their institutions I decided not to apply there. You could see by their body language and faces that they were negative towards me and the problems they could see for themselves. To simply reject my application removed the problem. I hope one day someone will stand up to some of them and appeal, or at least ask for detailed reasons for rejection. For me it was easier to go to a more supportive place and environment ... I almost got worked up then!

Q: Are there any areas of science that you cannot cope with from a wheelchair?

A: Yes, but I'm not afraid to ask for help if required. Other non-disabled also ask for help, don't they? Individual people must decide what they can or cannot do. After all they are the experts on their personal situation, not someone else. This can sometimes mean a bit of education for the organization concerned or the school careers adviser. It can also mean a need for a lot of 'stickability' by the disabled person in order to overcome the misconceptions of other people. I don't want to be a brain surgeon, if that is what you meant, but some less physically disabled might want to!

I particularly noticed that in the prospectus it indicated that the course was modularized, so if I have to go into hospital for a short while, I suppose I could forgo the modules that semester and pick them up again the following year when I have recovered? That's what I did for my A level, as it was also modularized.

The tutor had to think about that for a moment, as he could not remember anyone doing that before, but he had to agree that it was what the prospectus said, and the offer needed to be fulfilled.

After the 'analysis of courses and suitability of qualifications' was concluded and lunchtime approached, the conversation moved to the areas of disability. The tutor hastily arranged for them to be joined by someone from the student support service to give advice about disability matters, social service support, university regulations, financial support and personal support needed, and so on. Decisions were then made jointly about processing the application further should it arise.

Teaching staff responsibilities; safety matters

It is probably true to say that the majority of staff, and particularly staff in science, engineering and medical departments, have not had many students with disabilities attending their courses. Certainly in recent years there have been an increasing number of students declaring themselves as having the rather more hidden disability of dyslexia, but what about physical disabilities?

If a student is known to have a disability that will affect his or her work on the course, it is the responsibility of the course leader or year or module leader to inform the lecturers concerned. Many of the staff will not be overly familiar with what is available to them to support the student, so a briefing at the start of the year might be in order, together with a leaflet of contact people for advice, within both the department/faculty and the student support service. A brief set of photocopiable hints (see Hopkins and Jones, 2000: Appendix) is also useful to help to allay any apprehensions tutors may have.

One of the biggest concerns of staff is safety, particularly in laboratory and workshop-based courses. Read what Robert said when asked about his safety record in a laboratory.

Q: Were you safe in the laboratory at school and college?
A: I am. I've got to be, it's my life and future livelihood, and I give partic-ular thought to experimental procedures. There will always be accidents and unexpected events, but that's life, and the unexpected makes life interesting anyway. The most unsafe place for most people is in the kitchen, not the laboratory.

Generally disabled people are more safe, as they know their limitations and are inclined to be more deliberate and forward thinking when doing particularly unusual or extreme experiments or sporting/social activities.

In laboratory/workshop-based courses, all experiments must be vetted for safety, and a risk assessment made for each one. In addition, courses that involve field trips must be vetted by lecturers in advance of the proposed visit. If a disabled student is going to use a particular experiment, the person responsible for that experiment might need to make a note about any extra precautions that need to be taken. Because everyone is different there are no general comments that can be attached to all experiments to cover all eventualities. That is true for any group of students.

There might be a very few experiments that some physically disabled students will not be able to do, but that does not, of course, make them non-scientists. Indeed, other non-disabled students might not have the opportunity to complete all the experiments in a series either. Often students work in pairs or groups for some experiments, and this procedure is equally valid and can be particularly useful when disabled students are present. When it comes to discussion groups/tutorials, it is important that the tutor leading the discussion ensures that disabled students get their chance of being the chairperson, even if they have speech, visual or hearing difficulties. There is good advice in a book and article by Alan Hurst (1998, 1999), who points out the trend of increasing numbers of older learners entering higher education, and that some of these people also have physical disabilities. They may well be excellent students and highly motivated.

The Royal Society of Chemistry (RSC, 1998) and the American Chemical Society (Reese, 1985) have some guidelines for physically disabled people in laboratories. We suggest that if a student with a physical disability can enter a practical chemistry course, other subjects should hold no fears in terms of physical accessibility.

This is what Robert said about safety:

> If you can you cook and manage a kitchen ... and you can feed yourself ... then you have the ability to do practical chemistry, but even if some of these procedures are difficult, are you any the less of a person? Any the less a professional? Any the less a professional chemist?
>
> Yes, sure, I know my limitations, but that makes me a much safer worker than some of my colleagues who, to say the least, are often somewhat fool-hardy and flippant about laboratory safety. I cannot afford to be. Haven't you got people working with you that think they are immune from accidents and put other peoples life in jeopardy?
>
> My focus of work has changed since the degree of my physical disability has increased as I get older, but everyone's role changes during their profession; hasn't yours?
>
> Sure I'm disabled and always will be, but the most 'handicapping' things are other people's attitudes, and buildings.
>
> People often have a low opinion of people's abilities, and just because I cannot stand (or another person not able to see, hear or speak clearly), Joe public treats you as an idiot and either shouts at you, talks to you as though you were a child, or retreats and walks away.
>
> A disability does not mean you cannot think, reason or solve problems. You don't have to do outrageously unsafe experimental procedures to be a scientist.

An article entitled 'Beating blind prejudice' (Ying Hong and Nikhil, 1998) outlines how disabled people have to battle with people and systems around them. It shows how a blind person can also be a 'safe' chemist. The department of which one of the authors was head has never had a 'reportable' accident with any of the blind and other physically disabled students who have studied chemistry there. Non-disabled students have had accidents.

The Association of Disabled Professionals (ADP) (see 'Useful contacts') aims to combat the stereotyping of disabled people and also helps

employers with realistic advice. In our view, it is no good producing a graduate if there is little or no chance of him or her getting a job.

Some European/worldwide perspectives

It may be suggested that the advances made in the United Kingdom into
allowing academic rights and privileges to disabled people have been a little
way behind those in the United States.

During 1996–98 the EEC Helios project (see 'Further reading') was
involved with many aspects of ensuring access into all levels of education
and employment by disabled people. Each section of the very large project
made a submission and suggestions for European Commission policies to
ensure access into all levels of education. The project allowed the participants to confer in the various countries of Europe, and begin to see how
each country was operating its access procedures. Some of the Scandinavian
countries were well advanced in allowing access into higher education,
although it was clear that many physically disabled students had reached a
mature age before the system allowed them to achieve the necessary entry
qualifications. Some Belgian universities, and particularly Louvain, provided
well for their physically disabled students, as did some French and German
universities, but these were often the ones where there was great enthusiasm by individuals in high academic and administrative positions. It is
difficult to give a global picture for Europe, but a summary is included in a
publication from the Helios project (Helios, 1998). The project encouraged
the interchange of disabled students on study programmes between the
countries. The issues raised here are discussed more fully in Chapter 2.

Barriers to progress: a summary

Access to courses is a right for students with the academic abilities to
benefit from them. As with any prospective student searching for a place in
university, the disabled student will find it to be an academic rat race, and all
to do with A level grades and points or equivalent qualifications. One thing
in favour of anyone wanting to enter science or engineering is that it is
easier to gain a place, because many students are wary of doing the necessary school subjects of physics, chemistry, biology and maths. And of course,
once individuals have achieved the appropriate qualifications, they should
make it easier for them to get a job, whether they are disabled or not.

In our view, the major barriers for those with physical disabilities wishing to enter any suitable career are:

- Advice at school at the age of 14. Pupils and parents should not be put off by statements like, 'Do the non-practical subjects, it will be easier for you to do history than chemistry.' Our advice is that you do some research and find out possibilities. Use the World Wide Web if possible. Do not be put off an ambition by poor advice.
- A course admission tutor who says (albeit to him/herself only), 'We can fill up our courses easily enough without the hassle of having to cater for disabled students.' Be positive and seek advice from organizations such as Skill. Quote the DDA, but not too forcefully, as it may frighten (and thus deter) academic staff if they feel that the student knows more than they do.
- Find a course where you can be happy, and where assessments and modular patterns are flexible enough for you to take a semester off if hospitalization is required.
- Find out if the establishment has a students' services department to give advice on disability matters, and contact them before you complete a course application form: at least a year before, if possible. Look at their Web pages.
- You have found a course, completed the course and gained a qualification: now find a job! This is another minefield not tackled in this section through lack of space, but one simple piece of advice is to use the careers service extensively. Some have officers who specialize in advice to students with disabilities. Consult with the Association of Disabled Professionals (ADP) (see 'Useful contacts').

The greatest barriers to following any course or profession are other people. They often need to be converted, but after seeing a disabled student become successful, they are often the strongest advocates of accepting another student with a disability. Then, who knows, you might become an admissions tutor yourself and be able to influence policy and principles for entry to higher education. You may develop even higher ambitions, remembering that the Minister of Education in a recent Labour government was disabled, and so was President Roosevelt of the United States.

Finally, there are some good ideas in 'Study conditions and behaviour patterns of students with disabilities', a collection of papers and research from a conference subsequently edited by Meister (1995).

Traditional courses and modular courses

The traditional continuous linear course, where one term's work totally depends upon understanding the concepts of the previous term, and which ends with a single set of end of year exams, is now a dying pattern. In this model, if the physically disabled student were to miss one week or month, all might be lost.

Modular courses are now common in schools and universities, with assessments designed for each module. Also, the options allowed by module selection can mean that disabled students have the same flexibility as anyone else in deciding how to manage their educational pathway (though that flexibility might be significantly more important to them). If a particular engineering module involves climbing gantries all the time, the physically disabled student would need to seek out other possibilities (for example, an alternative computer-based module might be available).

In some British higher education institutions, what are called 'short fat modules' are popular. These modules are often taught intensively, in a very short period of time compared with other modules. They are becoming particularly popular for part-time students who are funded by their employers, who obviously want their employees to complete a course in as short a time as possible. However, courses involving these modules are not suitable for some disabled people as they can lead to fatigue and overload. If an HEI prospectus fails to mention that a course of study includes such modules, the HEI is arguably acting in a discriminatory manner, which has become illegal since the Special Education Needs and Disabled People Act came into being during 2002.

If illness or hospitalization becomes a reality for an individual with a physical disability, he or she should be able to 'pick up' the period away the following semester or year. Local authorities and university exam boards are usually very understanding about flexibility in assessment patterns, hand-in dates for work, alternative assignments and so on where legitimate reasons apply, and especially where physically disabled students are concerned. We would suggest that all such things are possible without a necessary diminution of standards.

This chapter has only begun to tackle this wide subject, and further and more specific information can be found in other publications, including Hopkins and Jones (2000), and also the accompanying video of apparatus and equipment used in teaching chemistry with a range of disabled students.

References

Helios (1998) *European Guide of Good Practice: Towards equal opportunities for disabled people*, European Commission, Brussels

Hopkins, C (work in progress) Entry to Engineering Project 2000: A 12 month project based at Loughborough University Student Services, Loughborough, Leicester, to look at the issues around disability and engineering-based courses within British higher education. (Information from c.hopkins@lboro.ac.uk)

Hopkins, C and Jones, A V (2000) *Able Scientist/Technologist, Disabled Person*, Eslek, Long Whatton, Leicester (publication and accompanying video are available at £15 each from Eslek Publications, 36 West End, Long Whatton, Leics LE12 5DW, tel: 01509 843354, or e-mail: Ironsideuk@aol.com)

Hurst, A (1998) *Higher Education and Disability: An international perspective*, Ashgate, Aldershot

Hurst, A (1999) The Dearing Report and students with disabilities and learning difficulties, *Disability and Society*, **4** (1), pp 65–83

Meister, J (1995) Study conditions and behaviour patterns of students with disabilities, *International Proceedings of Conference at Tutzing, Germany*

Open University (OU) (1991) *Open Teaching Tool Kit for Disabled Students*, Open University Press, Milton Keynes

Reese, K M (1985) *Teaching Chemistry to Disabled Students*, American Chemical Society, Washington

Royal Society of Chemistry (1998) *Environmental, Health and Safety Committee: Note on disabled workers in the laboratory*, Royal Society of Chemistry, Cambridge

Skill (1997) *Skill into Science and Engineering*, Skill, London

Ying Hong, C and Nikhil, N (1998) Beating blind prejudice, *Chemistry and Industry*, **5** (1), pp 6–7

Further reading

American Association for Advancement of Science (AAAS) (1981) *Barrier-Free Laboratories and Classrooms in Science and Engineering: Resource directory of scientists and engineers with disabilities* (available from AAAS, 1333 H Street NW, Washington, DC 20005, USA)

Commission of the European Communities (1998) *Report to the European Parliament: On the Evaluation of the Third Community Action Programme to*

Assist Disabled People (HELIOS II, 1993–1996). Brussels, 20 January 1998. Com15 Final. (Catalogue No CB-CO-98-013-EN-C)

Corlett, S and Cooper, D (1992) *Students with Disabilities in Higher Education: A guide for staff*, Skill, London

Doyle, B (1996) *Disability Discrimination: The new law*, Jordans, London

HMSO (1995) Disability Discrimination Act, HMSO, London

Jones, A and Hopkins, C (2000) Able scientists, *Chemistry in Britain*, **36** (1), pp 42–43

Useful contacts

Association of Disabled Professionals (ADP)
170 Benton Hill
Horbury, West Yorks WF4 5HW
Tel: 01924 270335
e-mail: AssDisProf@aol.com

JISC (Joint Information System Committee for the Disabled)
Secretariat, Northavon House
Coldharbour Lane, Bristol
Tel: 0117 931 7403
e-mail: assist@jisc.ac.uk or jiscmail-helpline@jiscmail.ac.uk

Skill: National Bureau for Students with Disabilities
Chapter House, 18–20 Crucifix Lane
London SE1 3JW
Tel: 020 7450 0620
e-mail: skill@skill.org.uk
Web site: www.skill.org.uk

Skill Information Service
Monday–Thursday
1.30pm to 4.30pm
0800 328 5050 (voice)
0800 068 2422 (text)
Info@skill.org.uk

7

Issues for pedagogy (1)

Stuart Powell

Limiting preconceptions versus adaptation and innovation

Students with the visual and hearing impairments and physical disabilities mentioned in this first part of the book succeed in almost all areas of higher education. Jones and Hopkins give examples of students with physical disabilities successfully completing courses that in recent years would have been closed to them because of their disability alone. It is also clear from the evidence quoted by Roy (eg Richardson and Roy, 2002) that physical difficulties with hearing, vision and mobility do not have a significant negative effect on level of attainment. However, some subject areas attract more students with a particular impairment or disability than do others (for example, students with a visual impairment are more likely to choose computer science than architecture).

The issues for educators then are, first, how to guide choice of course without being constrained by any preconceptions of limitations imposed by condition, and second, how to think creatively about different ways of learning that can be employed to achieve the same learning outcomes. In this latter issue, the matter of adapting curriculum content and/or delivery becomes pre-eminent. Academic staff need to begin to challenge their own view of limits and their own view of what is required by way of participation in the curriculum to achieve a particular standard of performance, be that intellectual or physical. It may well be that innovative approaches or techniques are required to enable students to gain access to the successful learning that is possible for them.

Listening to the student

The point is well made in these three chapters that students are, in one sense at least, experts on their own condition and on its effects on their learning. It is important therefore for educators to listen carefully to what students say that they want and need in order for them to achieve at their maximum potential. Students arriving at the stage of higher education with the kinds of difficulty with vision, hearing and/or mobility described in these chapters will have learnt how best to negotiate educational processes. They have probably also developed an insight into what their teachers require of them by way of detailed information. For example, they will know what is best for them in terms of ways of facilitating lip reading, or they may be able to explain the level and kind of visual impairment that they have. (Of course, these remarks apply to those students who have lived with their physical condition for years, and throughout the phases of schooling that precede HE – the issues are different where this is not the case.)

The discussion of individual difference in the introductory chapter takes on significance here. Lecturers may well be meeting up with a visually impaired student, for example, for the first time. Certainly it is important for them to have information about visual impairment in general, but it is also important for them to be aware of the range of individual differences within the overall context of visual impairment, as discussed in the introductory chapter and again by Roy in his chapter. Lecturers need to learn to listen to individual students about their specific needs.

It may also be the case that these students have an insight into their teachers' motivation. Students such as these often come to understand quite clearly what forms of encouragement teachers need in order to rethink preconceived notions of 'disability' and begin to find ways of including them in curriculum planning. This is not to suggest that university lecturers lack motivation in terms of wanting to help their students with disabilities, but rather that they need to know about the kinds of things that they can do to facilitate the individual student's learning, and they need to be given exemplars of how successful that learning can be. In short, they may need to be shown possibilities. Nor is this to suggest that the onus for 'gaining inclusion' should be on the student. In the introductory chapter the rights and privileges of all students were explored. What is being suggested here is a need for a very real sense of negotiation and shared venture. One could argue, of course, that this should be the case for all students; however, for the students who require special teaching, this negotiation takes on more significance and requires a sharper focus.

University academics need to learn to ask their students in these cases for advice on their own way of teaching. A subsequent issue for lecturers therefore may be how to shift from being a teacher to being a learner. This may make them vulnerable, in as much as switching roles in this way requires a change in the power relationship. Negotiation between teacher and learner becomes a much more real and significant process when both partners in the negotiation bring new understandings to the situation, and where finding a way forward may require real changes to the usual procedures. Jones and Hopkins cite some examples where academic colleagues have very definitely not seen themselves as negotiators in this sense, and where prejudicial views have dominated early discussions with students, with negative effects. In Chapter 11 the issue of establishing mutual trust and openness at the outset of student/teacher relationships is revisited.

There is one caveat to the notion of treating students as experts in their own learning needs. It will be the case, as Jarvis and Knight point out, that some students have experienced school and/or home settings where their needs are very expertly met, and where they may have become, to a greater or lesser extent, unknowingly dependent on the expertise of their teachers and/or carers. When such support is withdrawn, students may experience disorientation where strategies that used to work for them (for reasons of context) no longer do so. Again, the issue for university educators is how to treat individuals as experts in their own needs, but at the same time recognize where they may not know about what they will require in the new and very different learning environment of university.

Students' prior experience

It was noted in the introductory chapter that students will come to the learning situations of university with their own individual set of prior learning experiences, which will have shaped their knowledge and the way they employ their skills. It was also noted that, while individual differences will make them unique as learners, some parameters on their development will give some commonality of experience. Jarvis and Knight point out that within the population of students with a hearing impairment, those with less hearing are likely to have been educated in a total communication or bilingual setting, whereas those with more residual hearing are likely to have been educated in an aural/oral environment. Again, it is therefore important for educators to recognize that, in this case, not all students with a hearing impairment will use sign language. In general, the issue for educators is to find ways of ascertaining individual needs within an area of impairment or disability. It is not good enough to know nothing about a condition, but neither is it satisfactory to assume that one description will fit all. It is necessary to recognize that the formality of a diagnosis can only tell so much. Each individual will come to the university with a distinct set of experiences, and to prepare for that person's continuing education in the university setting requires a detailed and personal history. Again, as noted in the previous section, listening to the student is paramount.

Planning

It is clear from the three previous chapters of Part Three that the need for planning before the student engages with the curriculum is of paramount importance. Where special materials (such as raised diagram copying) need to be prepared, extra time may be required. Where materials are obtained from organizations outside the university, extra time and perhaps resources need to be built into the usual notion of a preparation period. Where human resources, such as a note taker, are involved, again the organizational issues need to be resolved before the student begins the course.

Experimentation

Since we have argued for exceptional amounts of forward planning, it is also necessary here to note that staff and students together need to be prepared to experiment with situations and procedures in order to maximize the potential for success. Roy makes the point that there is a very strong sense in which all players need to be prepared to work out how best to proceed; he gives the example of taking notes, where the advantages of audiotaping a lecture for later transcription over a silent Braille device used at the time of the lecture need to be experimented with. Another example can be taken from Jarvis and Knight: that of lip speaking versus sign language interpretation. With the best of planning it will still be the case that students and lecturers find themselves in situations that are new to them, and where knock-on effects occur. Again, as noted in the introductory chapter, flexibility and an openness to change are of paramount importance. It is also important, of course, to recognize when things are not going well, just as much as to laud successes. Both parties (teacher and learner) need to establish a relationship in which honest feedback can be given and received in a constructive dialogue.

Involvement of peers

Jarvis and Knight make the point in their chapter that it is important for the success of inclusion for other students to be aware of the issues and to play their part. This is particularly true in the sense that communication is always a two-way thing, and because of the way in which much of university learning is in group or cohort mode, the role of peers becomes significant. For all students, peers are important in terms of influence and sometimes of support; for those with specific learning needs they may become an essential source of ideas and support. Certainly, peer groups need to be involved as much as the individual student wishes – respecting, of course, the individual's need for independence and choice over levels of disclosure (a topic discussed more fully in Chapter 11), as well as ways and means of peer involvement.

Success and failure

Jarvis and Knight open their chapter with an example of how close is the margin between success and failure for many students with specific learning characteristics. Not hearing the vital piece of the instruction means effectively that the student can work diligently and 'successfully' but not achieve what was demanded by the task. The potential for frustration and embarrassment is clear. The issue for educators is the need for special care in setting out tasks – special in the sense of recognizing the particular needs of the learner with regard to clarity. It is also necessary for lecturers to be flexible in their response to the kinds of 'error' that is described by these particular authors. In the example they give ('Choose a portrait artist') it is to be hoped that the lecturers concerned took a liberal view of the student's interpretation of the assignment. If they did not, clearly this particular student would have been disadvantaged through no fault of his own.

Reference

Richardson, J T E and Roy, A W N (2002) The representation and attainment of students with a visual impairment in higher education, *British Journal of Visual Impairment*, **20** (1), pp 37–48

Part four

Specific learning issues

8

Students with dyslexia and other specific learning difficulties

Stella Cottrell

Introduction

Definitions

In Britain, 'dyslexia' is often used in quite a general way to describe a range of specific learning difficulties related to underlying differences in processing sound, visual stimuli, symbols and movement. Sometimes dyspraxia (difficulty in coordinating movement) or dysgraphia (difficulty specifically with writing) or discalcula (difficulty with numbers) are separated out. In some counties many more fine distinctions are used to apply to particular combinations of difficulty and strength. It is not unusual for those with specific difficulties to experience two or more of these specific 'types' of difficulties; it is not yet really clear from the evidence how far these differently named conditions are part of an underlying broader syndrome, manifested in different clusters in each individual.

The term 'specific learning difficulties' (SpLDs) is sometimes used to indicate that a person does not find learning in general to be difficult. Rather, it is difficult to learn, perform or demonstrate knowledge and understanding under certain conditions for certain types of task. For this chapter, the term 'dyslexia' will be used most of the time as a shorthand to cover the broader range of difficulties. Although 'dyslexia' is a misnomer (it does not accurately describe the difficulties), using one term will make the text more readable.

The impact of 'dyslexia'

Difficulties and differences in processing sound, visual stimuli, symbols and movement impact upon tasks which require certain kinds of information processing, linear sequencing, timing and motor coordination. As a result, dyslexic people show unexpected levels of difficulties in performing, at will and with ease, one or more relatively basic activities such as writing or reading text, music, dance notation or other symbolic representations; spelling; basic numerical computation; organizational skills; listening; speaking; balance and coordinating physical movements (Miles, 1983; Sharma, 1986; Fawcett and Nicolson, 1994; McLoughlin, Fitzgibbon and Young, 1994). There may be particular difficulties in combining non-automated tasks (Fawcett and Nicolson, 1994), such as listening, writing and spelling in lectures or seminars, or speaking and writing up answers on a flip chart in a group exercise, or balancing the body while working out a problem aloud during practical work.

Generally, higher cognitive processing skills which characterize university study, such as reasoning, interpreting, understanding, creating and synthesizing, are not directly affected. Performance on higher level tasks may be indirectly affected if, for example, individuals cannot gain access to course material because they cannot process text by eye. In such a case, the dyslexic person is in a similar position to a partially sighted or blind person. Another dyslexic person might have difficulties in processing sound after a short time, and is in a similar position to someone with hearing impairments. A dyspraxic or dysgraphic person may not be able to produce writing at speed, and in lectures or exams, with respect to writing may be in a similar position to someone with a missing or broken limb. Some dyslexic people experience combinations of more than one of these difficulties at certain times.

Dyslexic people vary greatly in their level of performance, and include those who have developed exceptional compensation strategies (Cottrell, 1996a) and the very gifted (Aaron and Guillemord, 1993; Vail, 1990; Everatt, Steffert and Smythe, 1999). Some people with specific learning difficulties may demonstrate unusually high levels of mathematical, spatial, linguistic or creative ability. Dyslexic people can tend to excel in subjects such as engineering, architecture and design, and some have attributed this to the ways in which the brain may work differently in dyslexics (Miles and Miles, 1993; Stein, 2001). Higher order thinking tasks can be easier for dyslexic students than apparently simple tasks, and some find university work better suited to their abilities than school work. Rote or 'parrot' learning is particularly difficulty for dyslexic people, who tend to prefer 'deep understanding', and personalized and applied approaches to study. It is becoming well established in universities that being dyslexic or dyspraxic is not, in itself, a barrier to achieving the highest degrees (Cottrell, 1996a; Singleton et al, 1999).

From what has been described above, it should be clear that dyslexic and dyspraxic people tend to show unusual or unexpected patterns of strengths and weaknesses in learning and performance. Being dyslexic or dyspraxic does not in general mean that a person 'cannot' do something – given sufficient time, means and encouragement. Time is key. People with dyslexia who are capable of performing complex reasoning tasks at their own speed can fail on more basic tasks when working under timed conditions (Ellis and Miles, 1986; Seymour, 1986). It may take a dyslexic person much longer to learn and perform some of the more basic subskills of a task because of their processing difficulties, which can be experienced as extremely frustrating and embarrassing. Certain aspects of the environment may need to be altered in order to allow those with specific difficulties either access to information, or to reveal their knowledge and understanding. In this respect, dyslexia is similar to most other disabilities.

It is often not appreciated how hard and frustrating it is, and how much application is needed, for a dyslexic person to perform some of the more basic skills. Nicolson and Fawcett (1994) suggest that dyslexic children may take 10 times as long to learn some subskills. They found that dyslexic teenagers were more likely to be making errors after 10,000 trials on an eye–hand co-ordination task than non-dyslexic peers after only 100 trials (Nicolson and Fawcett, 1993); despite this, they performed as well as others a year later, after having had optimal conditions in which to learn. As a result of the unusual combination of difficulty and ability, dyslexic people have often received very mixed messages about being both 'very bright' and 'very stupid'. Those who are obviously bright may have a life history of being dubbed 'lazy' or 'wilful'. This can have long-standing effects upon their readiness to 'try again', to 'do what they are told', or to take other people's estimation of them at face value. There can be deep emotional scars (Edwards, 1994), and in some cases, predictable behavioural problems. It is not unusual for dyslexic people to show either very high or very low levels of endurance, motivation and application, depending on how they have responded to, and been supported with, their dyslexia. Dyslexia induces tiredness, and dyslexic people can be prone to working very close to their stress and exhaustion thresholds for long periods. Conditions that are commonly stress-related are again more common in dyslexic people (such as asthma, skin conditions, allergies, migraine, working memory difficulties and auto-immune conditions).

Explanations of dyslexia

While there is extensive research into minute details of dyslexic performance, there is not yet consensus on the underlying causes. Explanations are being researched at various levels. For example, there is research that argues that dyslexia is genetic and runs in families (Defries, Alarcon and Olson, 1997). Galaburda (Galaburda *et al*, 1987; Galaburda, 1993) and others have suggested there are physical differences in the brains of dyslexic people. These may result in neurological differences which, in turn, give rise to tiers of other interrelated effects (Frith, 1999). From underlying genetics and anatomy, differences may arise in the way the brain functions, resulting in unusual difficulties with some tasks, but also concomitant abilities and strengths (Stein, 2001). Difficulties underlying surface task performance have been linked with slow processing of visual, auditory and tactile information (Laasonen, Service and Virsu, 2001). Some research has linked dyslexia and attention deficit disorders to deficiencies in fish oils (Mitchell, 1987; Stordy, 2000; Stein, 2001). The Baltic Dyslexia Research Laboratory has found associations between dyslexia and left ear dominance, auditory processing anomalies and epilepsy (Johansen, 1991; 1994). There are other avenues of research that suggest alternative explanations.

Generally, it can be concluded that dyslexia is a complex syndrome that affects each individual differently depending on the specific cluster of difficulties each person experiences, compounded by the age at which support was first offered, the kind of recognition and support received, the coping strategies and behaviours developed to manage the difficulties, individual strengths, and the general and immediate environment that impacts upon performance. This makes it important not to overgeneralize from one dyslexic person to another.

However, complexities in the definition and explanations of dyslexia can distance us from the everyday reality of how dyslexia is experienced. In order to help the reader appreciate how dyslexia impacts directly and indirectly upon students at university, a case study is offered below. From what has been said above, it will be clear that the example of 'Selima' cannot be taken as 'typical'. However, it does illustrate issues that arise frequently. Selima's experiences will be used to explore the kinds of intervention that can be made to increase the possibilities of a more successful and enjoyable experience for dyslexic students.

Case study

Schooling

Selima was identified as dyslexic when she was 17 and struggling with her A levels. The additional burden of reading at A level overstretched her coping strategies to such an extent that her self-esteem plummeted. She was taken to the doctor when she became withdrawn and bulimic. The doctor suggested she see a psychiatrist. With some reluctance, her parents opted instead for a psychotherapist. In the course of therapy, Selima mentioned that she thought she was 'mad' as the 'print jumped about like ants' when she was reading. She had seen a film as a child where a person who apparently 'saw insects' was described as mad and locked up in frightening conditions. Selima was so terrified by this that she had guarded her secret of the 'ants' until she felt safe enough to confide it to the therapist.

From the therapist, Selima was referred to an educational psychologist, who described her as 'intelligent', with the 'cognitive ability' to do well at university, but with 'classic' symptoms of specific learning difficulties (dyslexia). Among her dyslexic characteristics he included difficulties manipulating information in working memory; difficulties with sequencing; very poor immediate recall of a series of graded reading passages (which she had found easy to read); excellent spoken English; excellent written English expression although with poor pen control and many self-corrections, minor errors and two missequenced spellings. Selima showed outstanding ability in visually based and three-dimensional tasks. The psychologist also noted early childhood problems with reading, with 'learning things off by heart', and persistent problems with mathematical tables and accurate copying of data. Despite this, Selima's school refused to accept the diagnosis, arguing that they believed Selima had language difficulties arising from being multilingual, and that her other behaviours were common to adolescence and attention-seeking. As a result, Selima did not receive any specialist support and received low passes for her A levels.

Entering university

By the time Selima entered university she had a rich history of dealing with 'experts' and of being referred from one person to another, each with different views of her needs, and of receiving little help for her learning needs. As a result she decided not to declare her dyslexia when she entered university, anxious in case she was asked to leave if lecturers thought she had problems. When she failed her first semester examinations, teaching staff suggested that she be referred for a dyslexia assessment. At that point she mentioned that she had been diagnosed as dyslexic; her lecturers were extremely exasperated. They felt she had deceived them unnecessarily as they had spoken positively about dyslexia assistance at induction; they could have offered her help and they felt her 'failure' reflected badly in their pass rates. Selima did then receive a wide range of support, including assistive technologies paid for through the Disabled Students' Allowance, individual and group study skills support aimed at dyslexic students, and amended assessment procedures, as well as some targeted support from her tutors.

Support

Selima was one of over 1000 students referred to the Learning Development Unit at the University of East London between 1995 and 2000. There are many aspects of Selima's story that will not be true of all dyslexic students. Not all find that text 'moves' or becomes distorted, although a significant number do (Wilkins, 1990; Irlen, 1991). Some will have received support all the way through school; others arrive at university with no idea that they may be dyslexic. The emotional impact of dyslexia is not as manifest in most dyslexic students as in Selima's case, but it is common for there to be a profound emotional impact upon learning. All dyslexic students bring a different combination of dyslexic characteristics, coping strategies, learning histories, family and professional responses that mean they 'live' their dyslexia in very distinct and individual ways, despite surface similarities. Nonetheless, Selima's story highlights many of the issues that face students with dyslexia.

First of all, Selima had lived for many years with a secret that she found terrifying to speak of, not least because it was intertwined with other myths and fears. It is not unusual for students to attribute aspects of dyslexia to a range of reasons that make sense to them as children. Usually these have negative connotations and are associated with events that caused them extreme embarrassment and shame (Edwards, 1994; Cottrell, 1996a). Even children assessed as dyslexic early, and who receive help, rarely enter university with an understanding of what dyslexia is or what it might mean for them as adults. This can result in a wide range of emotional and behavioural responses that, from the outside, can seem baffling to those who take a solution-focused approach to dealing with problems. The first need of dyslexic students at university is for those who teach them to be aware that there may well be both a difficult past and heightened emotional sensitivity that can act as a barrier to trust, to revealing the dyslexia, and to asking for help.

Strategies

Selima had developed strategies that had served her well up to GCSE at 16. Some students' strategies take them through A or even up to PhD level. For some, work placement rather than academic work is more of a strain, as it presents a range of unknown situations for which strategies have not yet been developed. Selima had found that textual distortions were reduced if she read in very dim light. Her reading strategy was to read a short passage then to make notes. This created a start–stop approach that meant she did not focus on the text for very long. The note taking helped her to remember what she had read. However, at A level she found that she had to read much longer texts and sections of text before stopping to take notes. If she read for more than 10 minutes, her eyes started to jump about the page, she could not track from one line to another, 'words ran off the page like waterfalls' or 'danced about'. Concentrating on following the text became increasingly difficult: nausea, headaches, or drowsiness ensued. She was also scrupulous in checking and rechecking her work, looking for errors and working on a computer so that she could spell-check. At university, her problems became worse as the amount of reading and writing increased.

Reading books remained difficult for Selima. She found skim reading very difficult. However, her support teachers trained her to use her time effectively to find relevant parts of the text with minimum effort. She then scanned these into her computer and changed the appearance of the font on screen, and either printed texts out or used a screen–reader to listen to it being read aloud. In Selima's case, simply double spacing text, ensuring it was no smaller than font 14 (Times New Roman, in her case), and printing it on any coloured paper was sufficient to lengthen the time she could read from 10 minutes to half an hour or more. In addition, her lecturers gave her copies of course materials on disc so that she could adapt them on her computer and print them out to read. This was the support that Selima said she appreciated the most, even though the adaptations were time-consuming.

Other students have found that changing the appearance of text makes little difference. A small number find that using coloured overlays can make a dramatic difference. One student who read by sounding out words slowly letter by letter was able to improve her reading instantly to almost normal speed for reading aloud when she used a combination of font size 26 in

Ariel, double spaced, with three dark filters laid over the top. About half the students referred state that colour filters can make a marginal difference to how long they can read without discomfort. Many dyslexic students ask if tutors can point out in advance the most relevant parts of texts. Lecturers are generally reluctant to do this, as they argue that part of academic training is being able to select for relevance. However, it would be useful for staff to practise selecting text under a flickering light, scanning material into a computer, redesigning the text on screen and printing it out again, reading it under a flickering light, to appreciate the additional time needed to complete a reading task with a disability, and the importance of offering the maximum possible guidance on where to locate essential reading. Some dyslexic and partially sighted students pay for readers to put text onto tape: as they cannot pay for every page to be read, guidance on essential reading can make the difference in students gaining any access to the material they need.

Selima was fortunate in receiving the Disabled Students' Allowance that paid for individual support to update her study strategies in line with the requirements of higher level study. This was made concrete by the assistant working from the specific examples of her own work, and modelling her understanding of required language structure (such as paragraphing) from correct and near-correct examples in her own work. With mature students, this model can be taken much further. Mature students with dyslexia often lack confidence in their ability, and have underdeveloped writing skills. Such students benefit from explicit coaching in how to transfer skills from everyday activities to develop academic skills. The 'expertise metaphor' approach (Cottrell, 2001) trains students to use apparently unassociated skills (such as dressmaking and car mechanics) to identify and transfer subskills to academic tasks. This builds confidence in their own abilities, and also explicitly trains students to 'transfer' skills and expertise.

Key learning needs of dyslexic and dyspraxic students

Students with specific learning difficulties are likely to perform best when:

- they can be creative;
- they are relaxed and confident rather than stressed and pressurized;

- they have sufficient time to work at their own pace, double-check their actions or output, and to undertake multiple practice in new tasks;
- they can pause, relax and focus before and during tiring or demanding tasks;
- they can plan out their task and compensate for their specific difficulty rather than being 'put on the spot';
- they are given time and space to work out how to perform a task 'from within';
- they have specialist guidance to identify appropriate personal strategies;
- they are allowed to demonstrate their understanding in the means that best suits their disability (variously, by voice, hand-writing, typing, voiced software, production of artefact, practical demonstration, etc);
- when they can make use of their best sense modality, such as sophisticated colour coding, auditory memory, or opportunity to move about and shift position;
- their attention is not diverted by unnecessary interruptions or distractions;
- visual (such as overheads/handouts) and sound (such as tape) stimuli are good quality;
- unnecessary hurdles are removed in due consideration for the additional time that tasks can take;
- verbal instructions are accompanied by written ones, and vice versa.

Pedagogic approaches

Responsive approaches

There is now a wide range of well-documented ways of responding on an individual basis to students with dyslexia. These were evolved by practitioners with students, primarily during the 1990s, and were drawn together and strengthened by the National Working Party on Dyslexia in Higher Education (Singleton *et al*, 1999). Case studies give the best impression of how the support available may be used in individual cases (Cottrell, 1996a; 1996b; 2000) A browse of university Web sites or Disability Statements will reveal a high level of commonality in the kinds of resource available. The kinds of support which dyslexic students can generally expect to be offered are itemized in the box.

Support generally available to dyslexic students in higher education

- An initial confidential interview or 'chat' to explore a person's concerns.
- Dyslexia screening.
- Free or subsidized assessment for dyslexia, if this is felt appropriate.
- An assessment of support needs for HE study (sometimes called a SASSA).
- Individual or group support by dyslexia support tutors.
- Recommendations for specialist equipment (for those eligible for the Disabled Students' Allowance).
- Assistance claiming Disabled Students' Allowances (most British dyslexic students are eligible).
- Access to computers and possibly to specialist software on campus.
- Additional time and possibly other consideration for exams.
- Marking processes which give some consideration for dyslexic difficulties with spelling, grammar and phrasing.
- Specialist support from counselling services, especially following an assessment.

Some universities offer a range of other services such as advice on choosing programmes; advice on presenting dyslexia to employers when applying for work placements and jobs; dyslexia-sensitive technical support or advice on how to contact specialist opticians. It is not uncommon now for lecturers to provide copies of lecture notes in paper or electronic form.

Ways that dyslexic students can help themselves

There are also many ways that dyslexic students could help themselves which they may not be aware of or which they can be reluctant to take up.

- Many students are not aware of the range of ways that IT can help. The dyslexia coordinator in the university can advise. For example, students can take control over written text by altering the size and type of font, line spacing, the colour of text and background, and make other changes to the text on a computer in order to suit their individual needs. Screen-readers on a computer can read text and even spellcheckers aloud to help identify what is written.

- Breathing exercises, some sports, and meditation can have a positive effect upon reducing stress and help students to manage the panic that can increase dyslexic symptoms.
- Many students feel embarrassed to attend counselling or assertiveness programmes that could offer the support and practical guidance they need to cope with their dyslexia over time.
- Students do not always make the best use of study support on offer. Increased self-awareness through discussion, guided activities, self-observation and reflection can help to identify methods of organizing study that can seem trivial and idiosyncratic but which may have a profound effect on improved performance or quality of life in individual cases.
- If one method does not work, another might. Students need to maintain the confidence to keep trying out different combinations of potential support until they find what works best.

Inclusive approaches

The situation of dyslexic students in higher education has changed dramatically between 1991 and 2001. Ten years ago it was hard to gain Disability Allowances for dyslexic students, few of whom gained support; many lecturers were uncertain that dyslexic students could really succeed at university. Few students revealed their dyslexia, and few lecturers would have known how to respond. While the situation is not yet ideal, the position in the opening decade of the new millennium is very different. The number of known dyslexic students has risen dramatically to almost 2 per cent of the student population, and is expected to rise further (Singleton *et al*, 1999). Now, most lecturers who have taught for a few years will have been asked to provide support for at least one student. In staff awareness sessions on dyslexia, the level of general awareness about dyslexia is apparent: lecturers are now much more likely to 'want to know more' than to say they don't know what dyslexia is. Questions from lecturers are more frequently about the finer details of support and on how to resource the wide diversity in need, than to argue about whether dyslexics belong at university.

In general, support for disability in HE during the 1990s was responsive in nature: universities provided services to ensure that individual needs were addressed. For dyslexic students more than for other disabilities, support was often generic to the students as a group. Even in 2001, dyslexic students tend to be offered standard time allowances of 10 or 15 minutes an hour for timed examinations, rather than amended assessment in tune with individual needs. Dyslexic students may receive IT solutions of a general nature, or receive copies of overheads and handouts if they are lucky. The 'solutions' offered result from the rapid rise in numbers and the paucity of expertise and resources, rather than the actual needs of each student. This is likely to continue for the foreseeable future.

However, there are strong forces encouraging universities to take more inclusive approaches to disability support. First, there are external imperatives. The QAA Codes of Practice (1999) and Special Educational Needs and Disability Act (2001) are both explicit that disability support should be regarded as an integral part of the work of all staff in a university rather than just specialist staff. The QAA Code refers specifically to teaching attitudes and methodologies. Second, information technology offers increasing opportunities to ensure programmes are inclusive from the outset. Materials provided electronically, for example, can be altered by students to suit their needs or combined with assistive technologies such as screen-readers that help some dyslexic readers. Paradoxically, if disability inclusiveness is not considered at the design stage for computer mediated and assisted learning, then disability discrimination can be greatly increased. Care has to be taken to ensure that materials are designed so that screen-readers (or Braille machines or other assistive technologies) can interoperate with them (Hesketh and Martin, 2001). Finally, there is a growing awareness by teaching staff that some of the support strategies suggested for dyslexic students are useful more generally, enhancing the learning experience of all students.

A few examples can serve to illustrate the importance of inclusive practices to enhancing the experience of both dyslexic students and their peers. Dyslexic students may, for various reasons (such as hearing anomalies, lack of automaticity when writing, or attentional difficulties), find it difficult to 'catch' new or specialist vocabulary. They describe being 'stopped in their tracks', suddenly unable to remember a familiar word like 'the' or 'who', even though they have just written a more complex phrase perfectly. This can disrupt their attention disproportionately, so that they miss chunks of a lecture and their notes may not make sense. Sound-sequencing difficulties associated with dyslexia can make it impossible for some dyslexic students to look up a word in a dictionary if they fail to copy it down from the board, or if they do not recognize a word when reading paper-based material. In other words, there are particular reasons related to a disability that a dyslexic student may need to have lecture notes provided, as well as glossaries of specialist terms and concepts.

However, if notes were made electronically available to all students, along with glossaries, a wide range of other students in a class might also benefit. For example, international and multilingual students often state that lectures are a waste of time as they cannot follow what is said, and that their attention is so focused on listening that they take inadequate notes. Like dyslexic students, multilingual students struggle to make sense of dates and numbers when they receive these by ear, and they tend to translate these back to their first language in order to make sense of them. This disrupts concentration, and the students miss chunks from taught sessions. Students who have been out of education for a number of years, especially those who left school early, can find it difficult to write at speed and catch all of a lecture in notes. They may also have to pause to consider spellings because of recent under-use or poor initial schooling. The effects of word processing on writing speed in the general student population is still not known. However, there are support structures in the USA, and in some British universities, such as the 'Supplemental Instruction Scheme', which are constructed on the premise that students will not individually have a complete set of lecture notes. In recognition of these 'gaps' in access, more lecturers are making lecture notes available electronically, to ensure that complete access to the programme material is a basic starting point for all their students.

Practical things that lecturers and programme designers can do

The following list is indicative rather than exhaustive.

- Be aware of the potential for a wide range of undisclosed learning need and unknown levels of disability in any classroom.
- Set up an atmosphere where it feels safe for students to disclose difficulties, discuss different approaches and share strategies.
- Encourage students to work to their learning styles, and teach to a variety of sense modalities (see Cottrell, 2001).
- Provide lecture notes in advance, in paper and electronic form.

Include the main points and guidance on where to go for supplementary information.

- Offer glossaries of key terms and concepts.
- Give annotated reading lists so that those using personal readers or IT can use their time or funds to best effect in covering the essential passages first. Suggest alternatives in case your first recommendations are unavailable or will not scan into the computer.
- Offer alternatives to timed examinations where possible.
- For exam questions, avoid complex syntax and use of 'negatives'. Dyslexic students are more likely to use global reading strategies than word-by-word reading; they may not 'see' words such as 'not' and 'no' under exam conditions. In everyday life, they might use strategies to ensure accurate reading that are not possible under exam conditions.
- Use assessment methods that really allow students to demonstrate understanding and knowledge, with reduced emphasis on memorizing; dyslexic students find it harder than others to rote learn and to recall information such as names, dates and data under exam conditions. (This is one of the criteria used by many psychologists when identifying dyslexia.)
- Use assessment methods that challenge all students to demonstrate understanding, rather than allow clever use of English to mask ignorance. Dyslexic students are less likely to be able to use language to disguise what they do not know.
- Offer training and guidance on how to approach early assignments, as well as study skill strategies. These often work best if presented as 'professional' skills rather than study skills.
- Be aware that assistive technologies such as electronic readers or spellcheckers may provide only part-solutions and can be time-consuming.
- Ensure photocopies and hand-outs are of good enough quality to be scanned into computers. Avoid small font and cumbersomely arranged enlarged text.
- To help readability for dyslexic students, where possible, print text in columns, double spaced in Ariel 14.

Principles for successful educational experiences

Certain principles for providing a successful learning experience for students with specific learning difficulties are implicit in what has been described above. The first is recognition of the individual nature of the experience of his or her specific difficulties for each student. 'Specific learning difficulties' includes a broad spectrum of characteristics, strengths as well as weaknesses, usually experienced in clusters. From this we can derive a second principle, that a single solution is unlikely to suit all students. The strengths of one student (such as outstanding capacity to process visual information) may be the chief difficulty of another student. Where one dyslexic student may read by spelling aloud each letter, another student may find all sound processing to be exhausting. Where one dyslexic student learns best from discussion, another learns best from being left alone to sort out his or her own way of understanding the problem 'from the inside'. While many dyslexic students can be very practical, dyspraxic students may find even the simplest motor coordination takes an extreme amount of concentration, leading to exhaustion. Students with specific learning difficulties, in this respect, show a more exaggerated form of the diversity inherent in any group of learners.

The third principle is the importance of allowing students with specific learning difficulties the opportunities to develop appropriate strategies for each context. While most students can compensate for teaching method-ologies that do not suit their learning preferences, students with specific learning difficulties are more reliant on developing very sophisticated coping strategies to compensate for their areas of weakness. This often results in unusual areas of strength as well as creative problem solving borne out of necessity. Typically, the coping strategies required will mean working to their preferred sense modality (sound, sight, touch, movement), reducing stress and distraction, and needing more time to perform certain aspects of a task.

It is important to understand the value of 'time' to people with specific learning difficulties. The reasons time is an issue will vary in each case. For most, extra time is needed to focus the mind appropriately (a dyslexia equivalent to 'the zone' for sports people); for others, it will be because the physical process of reading is exhausting, requiring levels of attention or physical discomfort that cannot be sustained over extended periods without breaks; for others it may be because they perform motor tasks very slowly and with high levels of error. Others need a time delay of several days to be able to see what they have actually produced on paper rather than seeing only their intended output. Others need additional time because they read by ear (from tape or screen-readers) which is much slower than by eye. Most dyslexic students have difficulties with proof-reading, and may have to use several different time-consuming methods to arrive even at an approximately accurate text. Recalling specific data at speed can be an issue for many dyslexics. Delays in word recall, or poor motor control of mouth parts, can lead to a variety of speech difficulties which can mean that speech output takes longer. It takes most dyslexic people longer to organize concepts and activity out of the global integrated network of their thoughts into the linear sequence required for speech or writing (though not necessarily for sign language or diagrams). There are many other reasons where time is an issue; for most students with specific learning difficulties, several of these will apply. The addition of half an hour to examination time is unlikely to 'level the playing field'. For many dyslexic students, additional time meets a psychological and symbolic need, or a necessary safety net, rather than being an accurate measure of learning need.

Although individual difference will need to be acknowledged much more than it is at present in order to accommodate specific learning difficulties, perhaps paradoxically, it is by aiming at an inclusive curriculum that the needs of all are more likely to be met (Silver *et al*, 1988). While the needs of individuals must be considered, and there will be increased emphasis on this under the new legislation and QAA Code of Practice (2001), there is likely to be an increased emphasis on multiple modes of delivery and non-remedial patterns of support. Developments in tech-nology make this all the more achievable, at least in principle. As distant, flexible and technology-assisted learning become more extensive, there is increasing emphasis on programme material being made accessible to students through Web pages, as well as the development of electronic methods of supporting learning and encouraging mutual student support and collaboration. In addition the increased emphases on skills develop-ment, personal planning, vocational and practical work-based education are likely to mean that university environments will cater to a wider variety of students.

Conclusion

The situation for students with specific learning difficulties in HE has shown a dramatic change in the last decade. While there is still a long way to go to make HE completely 'dyslexia-friendly', most universities now offer a similar range of at least basic support facilities and amended assessment conditions. Disability legislation will contribute to further improvements. Moreover, there are dynamic changes afoot in the HE sector, with an increased emphasis on innovation in teaching and learning, new technologies, vocational education, skills development, personal action plans towards individual goals, and support to enable personal needs to be addressed. The concept that everybody has learning needs is one that can be used to positive effect in reinforcing support structures (as is indeed happening in some universities already). This can be conducive to promoting approaches to learning 'needs' that enable dyslexic students to address their strengths and weaknesses in a more inclusive and positive way. For students selecting universities in the future, the important questions to ask will not be 'What additional support is available?' but 'What kind of curriculum, teaching and assessment methods are used?' Students will need to know what attitudes to learning a university promotes, and whether or not these lead to the kind of positive learning environment where people with specific learning difficulties are not only helped to cope – but can develop their potential and thrive.

References

Aaron, P G and Guillemord, J-C (1993). Artists as dyslexics, in *Visual Processes in Reading and Reading Disabilities*, ed D M Willows, R S and E Corcos, pp 393-415, Erlbaum, Hillsdale NJ

Cottrell, S M (1996a) Lexically proficient dyslexic students in higher education, in *Second International Conference on Dyslexia in Higher Education. Learning Along the Continuum*, ed J Waterfield, Devon

Cottrell, S M (1996b) Supporting students with specific learning difficulties, in *Opening Doors: Learning support in higher education*, ed S Wolfendale and S Corbett, Cassell, London

Cottrell, S M (2000) Dyslexia into the universities, paper presented at Including the Excluded: International Special Education Congress, Manchester, 2000. [Online] http://www.isec2000.org.uk/abstracts/papers_c/cottrell_1.htm

Cottrell, S M (2001) *Teaching Study Skills and Supporting Learning*, Palgrave, Basingstoke

Dearing, R (1997) *Higher Education in the Learning Society: Report of the Committee of Inquiry into Higher Education*, DfEE, London

Defries, J C, Alarcon, M and Olson, R (1997) Genetic aetiologies in reading and spelling difficulties, in *Dyslexia: Biology, cognition and intervention*, ed C Hulme and M Snowling, pp 20–37, Whurr, London

Edwards, J (1994) *The Scars of Dyslexia: Eight case studies in emotional reactions*, Cassell, London

Ellis, N C and Miles, T R (1986) A lexical encoding difficulty I: experimental evidence, in *Dyslexia Research and its Application to Education*, ed G T Pavladis and T R Miles, Wiley, Chichester

Everatt, J, Steffert, B and Smythe, I (1999) An eye for the unusual: creative thinking in dyslexics, *Dyslexia*, **5** (1), pp 28–46

Fawcett, A J and Nicolson, R (eds) (1994) *Dyslexia in Children: Multi-disciplinary perspectives*, Harvester Wheatsheaf, Hemel Hempstead

Frith, U (1999) Paradoxes in the definition of dyslexia, *Dyslexia*, **5** (4), pp 192–214

Galaburda, A M (1993) Neurology of developmental dyslexia, *Current Opinion in Neurobiology*, **6**, pp 71–76

Galaburda, A M, Corsiglia, J, Rosen, G D and Sherman, G F (1987) Planum temporal asymmetry: reappraisal since Geshwind and Levitsdky, *Neuropsychologia*, **25**, pp 853–68

Hesketh, I and Martin, N (2001) *Betsie and Bobby go to the Virtual University: An interim report on accessibility developments in screen based delivery and assessment within the University of Luton*, ALT-C 2001, Edinburgh.

Irlen, H (1991) *Reading by the Colours*, Avery, New York

Johansen, K V (1991) *Diagnosing Dyslexia: The screening of auditory laterality*, ERIC, Indiana University

Johansen, K V (1994) Differential diagnosis and differentiated, neuropsychological treatments of dyslexia in *Legasthenie. Bericht über den Fachkongress 1993*, Bundesverband Legasthenie, Berlin

Laasonen, M, Service, E and Virsu, V (2001) Cross-modal temporal processing in adult developmental dyslexia, paper presented to the Fifth BDA International Conference, *Dyslexia: At the Dawn of the New Century*, York, 2001

McLoughlin, D, Fitzgibbon, G and Young, V (1994) *Adult Dyslexia: Assessment, counselling and training*, Whurr, London

Mitchell, E A (1987) Clinical characteristics and serum essential fatty acids levels in hyperactive children, *Clinical Pediatrics*, 26, pp 406–11

Miles, T R (1983) *Dyslexia: The pattern of difficulties*, 2nd edn, Whurr, London

Miles T and Miles, E (1993) *Dyslexia. A hundred years on*, Open University Press, Milton Keynes (first published 1990)

Nicolson, R I and Fawcett, A J (1993) Children with dyslexia automatise temporal skills more slowly, *Annals of the New York Academy of Sciences*, 682, pp 390–92

Nicolson, R I. and Fawcett, A J (1994) Reaction times and dyslexia, *Quarterly Journal of Experimental Psychology*, 47A, pp 1–16

Poustie, J (1998) Dyspraxia and the specific learning difficulty profile, in *The Dyslexia Handbook*, ed J Jacobson, British Dyslexia Association, Reading

Quality Assurance Agency for Higher Education (QAAHE) (1999) *Code of Practice for the Assurance of Academic Quality and Standards in Higher Education, Section 3: Students with disabilities*, QAAHE, Gloucester

Seymour, P H K (1986) *Cognitive Analysis of Dyslexia*, Routledge & Kegan Paul, London

Sharma, M C (1986) Dyscalculia and other learning problems in arithmetic: a historical perspective, *Focus on Learning Problems in Mathematics*, **8**, (3,4), pp 7–45

Silver, P, Bourke, A and Strehorn, K (1988) Universal Instructional Design in HE: An approach for inclusion, *Equity and Excellence in Education*, 31, pp 47–51

Singleton, C, Cottrell, S M, Gilroy, D *et al* (1999) *Dyslexia in Higher Education: Policy, provision and practice*, Report of the National Working Party on Dyslexia in Higher Education, University of Hull, Hull

Stein, J (2001) The magnocellular theory of developmental dyslexia, *Dyslexia*, **7** (1) pp 12–36

Stordy, J B (2000) Dark adaptation, motor skills, docosahexaenoic acid and dyslexia, *American Journal of Clinical Nutrition*, **71**, pp 323–26

Vail, P L (1990) Gifts, talents and the dyslexias: wellsprings, springboards and finding Foley's rocks, *Annals of Dyslexia*, **40**, pp 3–17

Wilkins, A (1990) *Visual Discomfort and Reading*, MRC.APU, Cambridge

Further reading

For students

Cottrell, S M (1999) *The Study Skills Handbook*, Palgrave, Basingstoke. This was developed for all students but is based on the experiences of several hundred dyslexic students.

Nosek, K (1997) *Dyslexia in Adults: Taking charge of your life*, Taylor Publishing, Dallas, Texas. This addresses in a practical way the emotional issues that many dyslexic people will recognize.

For university staff

Cottrell, S M (2001) *Teaching Study Skills and Supporting Learning*, Palgrave, Basingstoke. This includes both background information on developing inclusive support frameworks and practical advice on running sessions for individuals, groups or classes, on a range of study skills and related themes.

Hesketh, I and Martin, N (2001) *Betsie and Bobby go to the Virtual University: An interim report on accessibility developments in screen based delivery and assessment within the University of Luton*, ALT-C 2001, Edinburgh.

Wolfendale, S and Corbett, S (1996) *Opening Doors: Learning support in higher education*, Cassell, London. This covers a wide range of themes on developing inclusive environments.

General background

Frith, U (1999) Paradoxes in the definition of dyslexia, *Dyslexia*, **5** (4), pp 192–214. This draws together research on dyslexia.

Miles, T R and Miles, E (1993) *Dyslexia. A hundred years on*, Open University Press, Milton Keynes. First published 1990. An easy to read but comprehensive view of the development of our understanding of dyslexia.

Contacts

Adult Dyslexia and Skills Development Centre
5 Tavistock Place, London, WC1H 9SN

Adult Dyslexia Organisation
336 Brixton Road, London SW9 7AA
e-mail: Dyslexia.hq@dial.pipex.com

British Dyslexia Association (BDA)
98 London Road, Reading, Berkshire RG1 5AU
Tel: 0118 966 8271
Web site: http://www.dur.ac.uk/~dot7da/Web_e-dres/links.html
Equipment Resource Directory at http://www.equipservices.hefce.ac.uk

9

Overseas learners of English in higher education

Tim Parke

Overview

In this chapter I begin with an overview of two main ways in which overseas students coming into higher education in the United Kingdom are likely to have gained their knowledge of English at the point of entry, and follow this by examining the consequences of these processes for their subsequent discipline-based learning. I then examine some difficulties inherent in the varieties of English these students are likely to meet as they become involved in academic and social communities. This leads to an analysis of the typical activities taking place in discipline-based classes, both lectures and other sorts, looking at tutor and student expectation in terms of both language itself and classroom roles, and drawing some conclusions for the design and delivery of the curriculum. I then look at the additional classes – 'language support' – that these students may undertake, which are designed to complement and assist their studies, and at what they can reasonably be expected to do; and end with a brief account of recent technological developments that can assist language learning.

Two types of language learning

It is worth retaining a distinction between two broad types of language-learning procedure, and for two main reasons. One is that students coming to the United Kingdom have acquired their English in either one mode or the other, and the consequences will become evident to, and have implications for, those who teach them. The other is that such students can usefully be seen as in transition from one type of learning to another, and noticing the difficulties of this transition can be a source of insight to the teacher and thence to the student.

Broadly speaking, languages can be acquired naturalistically or in tutored settings (Ellis, 1997: 79ff; Cammish, 1997: 144). In the former condition, students find themselves for a specified period in the target or host country, and are obliged to pick up the language opportunistically in order to survive. It is the position in which some tourists find themselves when they visit a country whose language they do not know, and, wishing to communicate to achieve certain short-term aims, use every effort to break into the code going on around them to do so. Thus they notice and retain certain words that occur in the same context, they learn to 'read' a small number of useful labels (such as public signs), they become adept at asking native speakers to repeat things, they rapidly develop a gestural system which is locally understood, and so on. There is a pressure from within the individual to communicate for the satisfaction of immediate needs, and effective action and progress in language learning can both be gained in this way.

In the other situation, students will have attended a regular course of study. They have probably had the benefit of a teacher, materials, regular class hours, assessments, literacy, structured practice and everything else that modern pedagogy can devise. There is likely to have been a range of varied impulses to communicate as, naturally, different teachers put more or less pressure on students to communicate in the classroom, and in any case students can be adept at resisting or subverting this pressure, either because they do not see it as an effective language-learning strategy, or because they feel embarrassed.

There are advantages and disadvantages in each of these learning conditions, and their results can be noticeably distinct. One result of the first, naturalistic condition, is for learners to develop a set of strategies for breaking into the communicative code. They will have learnt, for example, to note words that recur frequently, and to recall the context in which those words occur, as this is a reliable guide to meaning. They may have written down certain key words in a rudimentary phonetic script so as to be able to retrieve and use them later. And they are likely to have remembered set phrases, or chunks of language, which it is useful to spiel out as fixed pragmatic units at the appropriate circumstances, and which enable a novice to pass in certain situations as a competent member of the language-using community.

The advantages of this kind of learning are clear: it is experiential learning, it is realistic, it is grounded in using language to do things, it involves real communication. And there is good evidence to suggest that learners who engage in genuine communication actually learn quicker than learners who spend most of their time in artificial activities (Klein, 1986: 50). But there are also clear drawbacks. The language systems acquired by such learners are likely to be fragmented and unsystematic. Learners may know a number of highly effective phrases that function well in set situations, but may well be unable to generate from them new utterances that work in new situations. The underlying patterns of the language may remain invisible, so that learning new language takes place as a series of discrete experiences, with no overall set of frameworks of existing knowledge, subsystems or routines at whose service new language can be put. In this condition, learners are subjected to an onslaught of language and fail to make holistic sense of it. They have to deal simultaneously with novel sounds, grammar, vocabulary, to say nothing of how language is used in context, which is reflected in, for example, differences of apparent politeness, of forms of address, and so on. A result of this information overload can be that the capacity to generate new utterances remains underdeveloped.

If we turn now to the second condition, we find, predictably, the reverse position. Students who have been exposed solely to classroom activities that are contrived and artificial experience a sense of unreality in the process that does little to favour learning. Traditionally, a classroom diet may feature such familiar exercises as repeating material chorally after the teacher, creating written sentences on a model from the textbook, completing blanks in written exercises, and asking one's neighbour where she lives. In addition, they are likely to have acquired an explicit set of rules for the formation of sentences, along with a specialist vocabulary in which to talk about those rules. In this 'tutored' condition, the learners, so far from being overwhelmed by language coming at them from every angle, have language broken down by the teacher (and the textbook, the curriculum, the exam syllabus ...) into convenient slices. For example, a class will be explicitly labelled 'pronunciation practice', or 'phrasal verbs'. In this condition, the learner can give explicit attention to separate areas of the language, and focus on one at a time.

In addition, the cline of difficulty is evident: students expect more advanced work to be more demanding than earlier work, and this expectation is usually met as they progress through a syllabus. Given the occurrence of repeated patterns in languages, the student will also meet with repeated instances of the same thing, which reassures the student by confirming existing knowledge, and eases the burden of continually learning something new. However, the drawbacks are there too. For all the acquisition of rules and a metalanguage, and learning lists of vocabulary, and focus on separate areas of language, can the student actually deploy the resources in real-life situations? Is the knowledge available for use? (Widdowson, 1989). It may only be in certain conditions, such as in written coursework, that the student will be able to organize language in such a way as to devise well-formed utterances drawing on classroom knowledge.

It is likely that most students coming to the UK for their higher education will have learnt most of their English in a tutored setting. The importance of the foregoing section is that higher education tutors are likely to see them as they emerge from that type of learning into another: into the informal settings of student life and everyday experience. That is, they may have to cope with three sets of circumstances:

- the change to a new type of academic tuition (in their discipline);
- the change from the language of the classroom to the new, informal language of contemporary British life;
- the change to a new type of English language tuition.

Inherent difficulties of language itself

I turn therefore to some of the inherent difficulties of the types of English such students are likely to meet.

Spoken English

The difficulties of adapting to spoken English as used in Britain are broadly threefold: problems of vocabulary, pronunciation and pragmatics.

Problems of vocabulary are initially puzzling for these students, but are quickly overcome. They can derive from a number of sources. The development of so-called 'World Englishes' over the past 30 or more years (Kachru, 1986) has seen the expansion of English as a language of wide communication. A once intact national language was exported, largely through colonial adventure and trade, and became either a language of government and administration, or simply a language taught for instrumental purposes. In this process it naturally took on elements of the first language of those who learnt it (Devonish, 1986). It is generally accepted that all varieties of English use broadly the same syntax: the subject–verb–object word order is constant wherever English is used. Variation naturally comes at the levels of vocabulary and phonology. This means that words a student is familiar with may not occur at all in British English, because the concept itself is not known. The reverse is true: life in Britain will require familiarity with previously unknown concepts that entail new vocabulary. It is also the case that existing words in a student's vocabulary can have a different meaning in the UK (see Saghal and Agnihotri (1985) for some examples). So there is likely to be a degree of mismatch between existing and new vocabulary.

A second source of variation, linking both vocabulary and pronunciation, comes from the accents, dialects and informal varieties of English. (I take the former two terms here in the slightly restricted sense of regional variations.) Students who arrive in a locality where the local spoken norm is nowhere near Received Pronunciation (RP), and is not close to Standard English either, may initially feel alarmed and resentful, imagining that their whole course will be conducted in a variety that they are sure is not the prestige norm. There is certainly an element of adaptation required here, but it is dependent on groups' or individual students' degree of integration into local communities. Those who integrate closely need to make the greater adjustment, but this is not problematic, given that integration is itself the motivation.

The issue of informal varieties is similarly related to the level of integration. Cammish says, 'those students who integrate quickly into campus life often enjoy acquiring the colloquialisms and slang they hear around them' (Cammish, 1997: 148). Informal language is initially bewildering, but it is also inherently attractive, and after all represents a natural use of language for higher education students. Through it, overseas students can establish themselves as having a certain level of face validity, often a precursor of acceptance into a group. More problematic is likely to be the perceived speed at which native speakers talk: the fact that all languages proceed at roughly the same speed per minute, as measured by the number of individual sounds spoken, is no consolation to the bewildered student, for whom the problem lies in distinguishing the boundaries between one word and the next.

A third difficulty derives from the mismatch in English between manifestations of what turn out to be closely related words, but that, thanks to the stress patterns of English, have no apparent connection on their first hearing. On the page, the following words are closely connected and built up from a meaningful 'core':

photo
photograph
photographer
photographic
photographically

Said aloud, however, they have only occasional similarities. In scientific and technical vocabularies, where there is a high preponderance of Greek and Latin-derived terms, helpful connections between the written forms are belied by a variety of spoken manifestations. It is a factor tutors should consider when presenting new terminology that 'looks' connected but that may not sound it.

Finally we need to consider pragmatics, or how language is actually comprehended and understood in real contexts. It is accepted that the meaning of what a speaker says is critically affected by audience and purpose. A tutor who walked into a classroom recently vacated by students remarked, 'Rather warm in here.' The look of distaste on her face made it clear to some of her audience that a correct inference was that she found the room stuffy, if not actually offensively smelly. Such use of language is often justifiably seen as 'saying less than you mean': it does not seem to conform to the everyday principle of 'being explicit' (Grice, 1975). Similarly, directives and invitations in English tend to be very weakly phrased. A colleague was recently bemused that a group of international students didn't move a muscle when, standing at the foot of the library stairs, he suggested 'Shall we go up?' Utterances of the type, 'Would you like to show me your notes on the lecture?' may meet with similar inactivity, and indeed the whole use of these types of verb – modal verbs, used in suggestions, invitations and 'softened' commands – is a particular difficulty for international students.

Written English

It is readily acknowledged that the match in English between the sounds of the language and its spelling is poor, and we have already glanced at this problem in relation to word stress. English children commonly spend longer achieving fluent literacy than their counterparts learning a language in which this relationship is more regular, and for students coming from the latter type of background this evident mismatch can be troubling. One has only to think of the variety of ways in which the sound 'oo', as in 'through', can be realized in spelling to be persuaded of this:

through
coo
true
brew
do

Stubbs points out that English spelling gives some information about word meanings directly, as well as giving information about pronunciation (Stubbs, 1980: 46). For students coming from languages where the relationship between the sounds heard and the symbols used on the page is more regular, this can be puzzling. Tutors are naturally aware of these irregularities themselves, but it does no harm to make them explicit when presenting new terminology. It is also helpful to make the most of what the English spelling system does for us: that is, as Stubbs says, the same spellings are likely to have the same meanings. Thus the string 'synthe-', whether it is found in 'synthetic', 'synthesis' or 'synthesize', will always have the same core meaning, even though the stressed syllable varies.

Typical activities in discipline-based classes

We come now explicitly to the language activities that students typically engage in as part of their ordinary learning. Despite rapid technological change, the dominant mode of teaching remains the lecture, but lectures have changed – for all students – in two important ways. The first is the provision of course materials. Students expect a booklet about the course, often giving proposed learning outcomes, a week-by-week breakdown of the course, assignment details, and a bibliography. They expect a handout at each lecture, and this often usefully provides a structure for the input. Secondly, technological change has meant that lecture delivery itself has developed considerably over even the last 10 years. In line with societal change, lecturers have become much more aware of the potential of visual impact, and so PowerPoint presentations, slides and video clips have become commonplace. It means that students do less pure listening, and more looking and listening.

These two changes have great potential for overseas students. A handout that gives the structure of the lecture is obviously helpful. Headings and bullet points are key signals to the course of the lecture, and enable students to match spoken and written language, as well as indicating what is most important in the content. If the handout has been designed with language in mind, it will also provide a glossary of key terms, and perhaps definitions, or references to where definitions can be found. Examples of the term contextualized in a sentence are very helpful (as in, for example, the *Cambridge Learners' Dictionary*), as this tells the students not just the word's basic meaning, but how it is used within the specialist discourse in question.

There is a single, but complex, difficulty: the simultaneous comprehension and production of language. Note taking demands ideally that students process, edit, and produce language online: that is, that they understand what is being said, can decide on what is worth committing to paper, and can write that selection of the input down. This means in turn that there must be speech that is loud and distinct enough to hear and comprehend, vocabulary familiar enough to understand, the chance to integrate what is said with what is written down on a screen or a handout, the opportunity to decide on what is vital and what can be omitted, and time to write. Nesi (2001) has illustrated clearly the variety of styles of lecturing to international students that were common in one university across a range of disciplines (30 departments), and there is no reason to suppose her work is atypical. She set out with these questions:

> How fast do lecturers typically speak? How much of what lecturers say are students intended to write down? Does a fast-paced lecture necessarily pose a greater challenge to the student note-taker?
>
> (Nesi, 2001: 201)

She measured four variables. One was the lexical density of the lectures – that is, the number of 'meaning-bearing' words, excluding such items as articles ('the', 'a/an') and the verb 'to be', as a percentage of all words spoken. She also measured the number of words spoken (taking a representative five-minute excerpt as her base). Alive to the possible connection between lecture style and the level of student interaction, she also looked at the number in each audience and the degree of participation. She summarizes her findings thus:

> There is evidence, as predicted, of a link between speed of delivery and lexical density, with faster lectures tending to be sparser and slower lectures

tending to be denser. There is also evidence that lecturers produce faster or denser text when they do not expect their listeners to record much of what they say, and when they are not presenting new and complex propositions – when content is fairly predictable, for example, or merely anecdotal.

(Nesi, 2001: 216)

These are fairly optimistic conclusions, as it seems that the lecturers in question used professional intuition and experience to exploit a trade-off between speed and noteworthiness, between compacted or complex information and rate of speaking.

Nesi comments only in passing on the use of handouts (Nesi, 2001: 213); it may well be that how 'full' and 'useful' a lecturer perceives handouts to be has a critical effect on delivery. However, it is apparent from my own experience that providing a handout is not enough: students (all students) need to be shown what a handout does and what they must do for themselves.

Roles in the classroom

All students, UK, EU and overseas, arrive at their university with a well-formed view about how teaching is delivered, and some attention is due to the different models of how teachers teach that overseas students are familiar with. In this domain, caricatures abound. Cortazzi and Xian, for example, drawing on several years of research, put up some prevalent presuppositions about Chinese students, before going on to give a contrastive account of dominant learning and teaching patterns in China and the United Kingdom (Cortazzi and Xian, 1997: 78). However, a key difference between some overseas students' experience at home and in the United Kingdom is the degree of teacher-centredness of classes. There can be an assumption that teachers have more or less sole speaking rights, are the sole sources of knowledge, need pay relatively little attention to improving how they transmit that knowledge, and should not be put in the awkward position of responding to questions to which they may not know the answer. This in turn is no doubt an exaggerated picture, but I hope a recognizable one (see Macrae, 1997: 141 for a corroborative list).

Students who operate, whether consciously or not, on this model limit unnecessarily their participation in classes and may be seen by teachers as shy, inhibited or lacking in initiative, while in many courses the ability and willingness to challenge a point of view, to see what the evidence says, to form an independent assessment of data and so on, are highly prized. These verbal acts are typical of seminars and tutorials, when there is space for relatively small-scale interaction. For overseas students, it is likely that a fairly structured assignment of roles will be helpful in the early stages. A good way of doing this is to provide a 'script' for the class in the form of a handout, with an overview of the tutor's expectations for the class, clearly defined activities and timings, key vocabulary (preferably contextualized), and an allocation of time to summarize what has taken place. Having overseas students work in cross-language groups is an advantage, though this has to be handled sensitively (Cammish, 1997: 148).

Group work itself has become very prevalent in British HE, with proponents stressing the communicative and interpersonal skills it is rumoured to promote. From the perspective of the overseas student, it offers two significant advantages. One is simply that within a group, a dynamic develops, with individuals developing roles in which they may feel at ease. To some extent such roles are predictable: most groups can be expected to have a 'natural' organizer, researcher, presenter, maverick. Exploiting these roles which have evolved due to the students' own interactions allows students to play to their strengths, but above all allows natural patterns of communication to develop between them. The second advantage is that, from a language-learning point of view, these patterns are of themselves very beneficial. There is plenty of solid evidence to show that opportunities for natural communication, where the two participants have a genuine need to communicate with each other because they have a common time-limited task that has to be completed, promote the acquisition of language (Ellis, 1997: 48). To return to the initial distinction, elaborated in the first section of this chapter, between two styles and conditions of language learning, group work is an example of language being used for real purposes, with a focus less on language itself than on what can be achieved through it.

Yet, as would be expected, there are concomitant dangers. One is that errors may become 'normalized' and pass unnoticed within the group. This is all the more likely given the notorious tolerance of native speakers for errors produced by second language users (Lennon, 1991): with time, and with the normal accommodation all speakers make to differences between the speech of individuals, errors are simply no longer noticed. While this is good for internal group communication, once language 'goes public', emerging again from the group to be a tool for more general communication – reporting back to the class or the tutor – errors and atypical usages will again be noticed. In an educational context, it is rarely enough for language to be a tool used for successful communication: it is nearly always judged for its own qualities, along with the content it expresses. So while peers may ignore errors, tutors and external examiners will not necessarily do so.

On the other hand, tutors have two responsibilities here. One is to be alive to language errors in class, and either to correct them or to refer students to professionals (see below). The second is themselves to produce models of the accurate and acceptable language forms they expect of their students.

We come here to a last major point relating to language and roles, but one that raises larger questions of the content and delivery of the curriculum. It is a truism to say that a class of students forms a kind of temporary community, adventitiously brought together, sharing space, routines, learning practices and resources solely for the duration of a course. One of the initial challenges for the tutor is to encourage the development of that community, so that such things as routines, patterns of interaction and behaviours make the course of each class productively predictable for both tutor and taught. A way for teachers to foster this virtuous dynamic is to find a common set of shared beliefs, cultural allusions or forms of language, a recognized and shared linguistic and cultural territory in which all members of a class have equal rights to speak and state an opinion. Here, the content of what is said is less important than uttering the words them-selves: language is reduced to a small number of key phrases and colloquial fragments that evoke and stand for shared views and attitudes that do not get full expression. It is the language of the insider community, and it has the desired effect of rapidly establishing a shared world of allusion.

However this may increasingly be the shared world of only part of the class. Overseas students entering the English HE system may be nonplussed by cultural references of this kind. In extreme cases, they may feel excluded by a culture that is tangibly present but never fully articulated: they are in the position of the child to whom the adult joke is never explained. The serious issue then is the tension between the need for class members to coalesce into a working unit, and the danger of excluding those members who have a socialization different from that of the host community. The curriculum has to be articulated in English that meets three criteria:

- Comprehensible: it is not limited by cultural allusions, its meanings are transparent, and they can be articulated explicitly (for example, they can be looked up in a relevant specialist/technical dictionary, rather than a cultural encyclopaedia).
- Transportable: the English should be usable in a range of different contexts, including for example the student's home country; it should also be of a level of formality that suits contexts wider than that in which it was acquired.

- Allusion-free: the English should be shorn of local characteristics that constrain its accessibility within a particular context.

Language support

The discussion so far relates to discipline-based classes in which students are studying the subjects in which they have a committed interest. Alongside these, many overseas students also take additional language support (also known by a range of other names; henceforth LS), in which they are taught a mixture of language skills and study skills. These classes recapitulate some of the issues of teaching and learning that have already been raised above – for example, the expectations about models of teaching – as well having their own distinguishing features.

There are two main oddities to be found in LS, one structural, one curricular, which it is as well to acknowledge at the outset, as they impact on the student learning experience in that they inform how both students and academics view this provision. Structurally, LS is oddly distributed around institutions. It can be found in Modern Languages departments, in English departments, or in Linguistics or Education: it may constitute a unit of its own (for example the English Language Unit), or it may not be an academic unit at all, but a division of Student Support Services. Academically, it may be viewed with suspicion: it does not recruit students, but has them 'given' by other departments that do (and which have to meet targets). On the other hand, it maintains language requirements for university entry, such as TOEFL or IELTS scores, which are nationally advised (for example, by the British Council), and which may look like an unnecessary obstacle to recruitment.

Language support sits somewhat uneasily within a quality assurance framework, as its results are best measured by the extent to which subject external examiners do not recognize weaknesses of English in coursework and exam papers. Its greatest success would be to put itself out of business: if students learn well enough, the argument goes, they will no longer need to attend these extra classes.

These points are clearly related to the issue of the curriculum the students follow. Language support is outside their mainstream learning: it is an add-on, taking extra time (from the students) and extra resources (from the institution). Academic departments see its role as to teach English in such a way as to minimize the difficulties other academics have in delivering their (more important) curriculum. That LS may have its own, fully worked-out curriculum, based on what is known about how adults learn languages, may not be uppermost in other academics' minds. Above all, it remains outside the students' course or modular count: it is not taken into consideration when computing a student's progress.

The consequence is that LS is subject to a kind of academic pincer movement. It is seen by both students and teachers as an addition to an already busy curriculum, and at worst as peripheral to it. If classes are outside the assessment logarithm that determines a student's degree, the institution is giving the message to all participants that these classes are insignificant. Students apply to do courses in discipline areas, and not in English language; and they are fully aware that these classes do not 'count' in the final analysis. On the other hand, both teachers and students look to LS to provide solutions: both parties expect English language tutors to raise the students' English to a level at which they can cope with a given curriculum. Where students are recruited to an initial year of higher education with a thinly veiled implication that if they succeed they will be accepted on to a higher-level course, the pressure to 'deliver success' becomes palpable.

Rationales for language support

It is a cliché to say that language teachers know their students 'better' than teachers of other subjects. Much of the early stages of language teaching consists of exchanges between teacher and taught based on everyday life and family circumstances. To a lesser degree, this process continues at HE level. English language professionals tend to have their students work in small groups, where they can observe patterns of behaviour, performance and individual characteristics, and where they frequently witness moments of crisis in students' personal lives. They are able to direct students towards the sources of help for personal enquiries, such as problems of registration, visas, housing and so on. They can explain apparent vagaries of local or national behaviour, which can range from explaining the origins of Armistice Day to unravelling a piece of baffling regional dialect.

More than anything else, they know the stages of language acquisition, and this gives them an invaluable set of tools. A good team of ELT professionals also has at its disposal a huge spread of knowledge of many subject areas, which can be used to make connections with its students' disciplines. A lot of this is available in ELT textbooks, which remain largely unknown to discipline-based staff. It is not uncommon for students to make a first connection with an aspect of their discipline as a result of an LS class or tutorial rather than through the discipline-based class on that subject. A reading text in, for example, methods of industrial production, or labour relations, can be the means of entry into the subject for a student who has sat through a lecture in the area and understood none of it.

These form part of a more purely academic rationale for LS. There is another strong argument in its favour: the classes can become a supportive social network. This works in a number of ways. Overseas students tend to form a strong bond with others who arrive at the institution at the same time, and whom they recognize from an initial testing session or a pre-sessional class. Support classes may be the only forum in which they are able to maintain these links.

Second, the organization of the classes, with students frequently working in small groups or pairs, fosters the creation of a large number of informal social micro-networks. It is likely that every student in a given class will have worked with every other within a few weeks of the start of the year. In mixed-language classes in particular, this gives students an opportunity to cope with new and varied speakers, and make the necessary adjustments in their own production.

Third, the classes provide a forum in which almost any question can be asked: students ask tutors and each other about the institution, English life, travel arrangements, communication with home, living conditions, assignments, and virtually anything else.

'And fourth, the classes provide a kind of systematic underlay for the development of the students' English. In their discipline-based classes the focus, as we have already noted, is not primarily on language. Students grapple with English as a means of communication rather than as a means in itself. For some, this will be enough to ensure a good level of competence. But given the irregularities and vagaries of English, students are likely to find questions about the language itself arising in their minds: why does the final 's' in plurals sometimes sound like an 's' ('cats'), sometimes like a 'z' ('dogs'), and sometimes like 'iz' ('horses')? Why do some verbs change the vowel in the past tense ('come/came'), others add '-ed' ('play/played'), and others not change at all 'put/put')? This is not to suggest that students keep a running log of the oddities of the language, but rather that in LS classes they get the opportunity to develop a fuller conceptual understanding of the English language system, relating the parts they happen to come across in their other classes to the fuller and more explicit picture that underlies that more haphazard exposure. The more numerous and strong the connections they make in this way, the more secure their competence will be.

Technology and learning English

This final section examines briefly two recent technological novelties that can be seen as playing a part in students' acquisition of English: the Internet, and e-mail. For further discussion of the impact of ICT in general on HE, see Chapter 3.

One clear benefit of the Internet is to make available an unprecedented range of written resources, predominantly in English (Hawisher and Selfe, 2000: 9). Students can access an immense, ever-increasing set of texts of all types, from online journals dedicated to their own area of specialism to transient (but highly motivational) advertising hype. Beyond this, a large number of Web sites, largely US-based, claim to be able to assist students in learning English, with the main focus inevitably on developing written language. A recent survey (Drummond, 2000) suggests that this kind of resource is at an early stage of development.

Undoubted positive aspects of sites developed so far are accessibility, informality and speed of response. Students can log on to a site at any time, ask a teacher any kind of language-related question, and be sure (in the case of efficient sites) of a rapid response. Loss of face is never an issue, as it can be in face-to-face interactions: no question is too dumb or too elementary, and the teacher is endlessly patient (Brandjes, 1997: 1). Where there is a rich source of material matching students' interests and needs, they can move fluently from one page to another, gleaning information and making links from one topic to the next. This in itself provides valuable practice in skimming written text (Grellet, 1981), extracting what is relevant and discarding what is not, and in making connections between related topics and vocabulary. Specifically in online writing classes, communication is no longer a one-way process, from student to teacher, but also operates productively between students: 'Risk-taking ... may become more common as a student reads others' writing or receives regular, positive encouragement from the teacher and peers' (Brandjes, 1997: 1–2).

However, rapid feedback to student writing looks at present like the most productive form of online tuition, and is in any case subject to two caveats. One is that it is probably most effective when a student is engaged in a piece of writing that forms part of a regular course, and comes across a one-off problem that he or she cannot solve alone. Here, a rapid answer from an anonymous teacher may be just what is needed to unblock the writing process. The corollary is that this is not really tuition in the sense of a long-term structured learning procedure, and any student who is already receiving good face-to-face tuition would be likely to use the online version solely for this purpose: as an out-patient rather than a ward inmate.

Attempts to teach other aspects of language, such as how to take part in conversations, seem less useful. One site features a number of somewhat stagy dialogues, such as 'Making friends':

Jim: I teach mathematics at Willow Springs College. What do you do?
Thinh: I am a mechanic at Allied Diesel. I repair truck engines.
(http://www.eslcafe.com/book/mkfrnd)

Although a voice track is supplied, this amounts to reading comprehension on the screen rather than practice in conversation.

A very recent initiative from the BBC, however, 'Learning English', (http://www.bbc.co.uk/worldservice/learningenglish), a World Service development, has taken a more interesting approach. This sets out to present English through topics such as the news, work, music and sport. It is highly topical, and aimed mainly at the young adult market. To take one example, a page available in December 2001 featured Britney Spears in the role of anti-fur campaigner. Students can listen to an audio clip of an article, read a summary of it, then see the article on the screen. Key phrases are in bold print, with a glossary underneath; then there are links to other related stories, Top of the Pops, Music Directory, and so on. This seems to combine a traditional approach to reading and vocabulary support with the technological advantages of simultaneous audio, and instant topical links.

However, it is clear that with the level of enthusiasm most students show for e-mail, it has potential as a teaching tool, even when the learners in question are already on site. One already commonplace step is to set up a class as a user group, giving out class information, dates and times, assignment information and so on. This is already the norm in many discipline-based classes. Language support tutors, however, can go much further. While (as ever) face-to-face teaching is irreplaceable, we can build on the agreed benefits of electronic communication: students find it easy to use, are willing to communicate in this way, and can receive rapid feedback. There is the danger that tutors will become trapped in an endless round of replying to individual queries: units need to plan jointly the level and type of information they want to put out in this way, and especially the format, level and type of response expected.

References

Brandjes, L (1997) Teaching writing in a web-based classroom: a case study of Ted Nellen's 'Cyber English' class, [Online] http://www.mbhs.bergtraum.k12.ny.us/cybereng.lizcyber.html

Cambridge Learners' Dictionary, Cambridge University Press, Cambridge

Cammish, N (1997) Studying at an advanced level through English, in *Overseas Students in Higher Education*, ed D McNamara and R Harris, pp 143–55, Routledge, London and New York

Cortazzi, M and Xian, L (1997) Communication for learning across cultures, in *Overseas Students in Higher Education*, ed D McNamara and R Harris, pp 76-90, Routledge, London and New York

Devonish, H (1986) *Language and Liberation: Creole and language politics in the Caribbean*, Karia, Kingston

Drummond, J (2000) *ELT Writing and New Technology*, unpublished MA dissertation, University of Hertfordshire

Ellis, R (1997) *Second Language Acquisition*, Oxford University Press, Oxford

Grellet, F (1981) *Developing Reading Skills*, Cambridge University Press, Cambridge

Grice, H P (1975) Logic and conversation, in *Syntax and Semantics 3: Speech acts*, ed P Cole and J Morgan, Academic Press, New York

Hawisher, G E and Selfe, C L (eds) (2000) *Global Literacies and the World-Wide Web*, Routledge, London

Kachru, B J (1986) *The Alchemy of English: The spread, functions and models of non-native Englishes*, Pergamon, Oxford

Klein, W (1986) *Second Language Acquisition*, Cambridge University Press, Cambridge

Lennon, P (1991) Error: some problems of definition, identification, and distinction, *Applied Linguistics*, **12** (2), pp 180–96

Macrae, M (1997) Induction of international students, in *Overseas Students in Higher Education*, ed D McNamara and R Harris, pp 128–42, Routledge, London and New York

Nesi, H (2001) A corpus-based analysis of academic lectures across disciplines, in *Language Across Boundaries*, ed J Cotterill and A Ife, pp 210–18, British Association of Applied Linguistics/Continuum, London and New York

Risager, K (1998) Language teaching and the process of European integration, in *Language Learning in Intercultural Perspective: Approaches through drama and ethnography*, ed M Byram and M Fleming, pp 242–53, Cambridge University Press, Cambridge

Saghal, A and Agnihotri, R K (1985) Syntax – the common bond: acceptability of syntactic deviances in Indian English, *English Worldwide*, **6**, pp 117–29

Stubbs, M (1980) *Language and Literacy: The sociolinguistics of reading and writing*, Routledge, Boston and Henley, London

Widdowson, H G (1989) Knowledge of language and ability for use, *Applied Linguistics*, **10** (2), pp128–37

Further reading

Byram, M and Fleming, M (eds) (1998) *Language Learning in Intercultural Perspective: Approaches through drama and ethnography*, Cambridge University Press, Cambridge

Liaw, M-L and Johnson, R (2001) E-mail writing as a cross-cultural learning experience, *System*, **29**, pp 235–51

McNamara, D and Harris, R (eds) (1997) *Overseas Students in Higher Education*, Routledge, London and New York

Swan, M and Smith, M (1987) *Learner English*, Cambridge University Press, Cambridge

URLs

http://www.bbc.co.uk/worldservice/learningenglish
http://www.mbhs.bergtraum.k12.ny.us/cybereng.lizcyber.html
http://www.eslcafe.com/book/mkfrnd

10

Students with autism and Asperger's syndrome

Tim Luckett and Stuart Powell

Vignette

James is a young man with Asperger's syndrome who excelled in a narrow range of subjects at school where he earned the nickname of 'the little professor' because of his serious attitude to study, smart dress and precocious vocabulary. While the other teenagers in his class spent their spare time gossiping and fooling around, James preferred to read textbooks or write computer programmes. Following excellent A level results, James was keen to go to university, despite his parents' concerns that he might have difficulty with the 'common sense' aspects of daily life when left to his own devices. The professor who interviewed James for a place at university was taken both with his impressive knowledge of his subject, and by the pedantic way in which he answered questions.

Once accepted onto the programme of study, James began the difficult task of adjusting to unfamiliar surroundings, and the challenge of structuring his own days rather than someone else doing this for him. Unlike most other new students, James avoided freshers week social activities in favour of the university library. Because of his unfamiliarity with the library cataloguing system, he had to search for several days to find the various subjects about which he wanted to read. Since no one introduced him to the university canteen, he took to buying his food from the same takeaway every day, despite having to walk some distance from the campus to reach it. James' room-mate, a potential source of help, started to avoid him after witnessing 'odd' behaviour when James thought he was alone. In lectures,

James sat in the corner and appeared distracted. However, his coursework marks were among the best in his year. His grades took a dramatic downward turn at exam time, when he panicked under the pressure.

Introduction to autism and Asperger's syndrome

Autism is a complex developmental disorder normally in evidence by three years of age. However, the full extent of atypicalities may not become apparent until later in life, especially where individuals are very able (Rutter and Schopler, 1987). The diverse range of behavioural manifestations seen in autism commonly disorientates parents and professionals alike. Nonetheless, the disorder is behaviourally defined, in terms of a triad of impairments in social interaction, communication and imagination (Wing and Gould, 1979) often accompanied by a narrow, repetitive range of activities. Although several causal candidates are currently under investigation, no one biological cause seems to underlie all cases of autism. Current diagnostic criteria for autism are outlined in Appendix 1.

Lecturers and others who come into contact with individuals diagnosed as having autism or Asperger's syndrome need to recognize first and foremost that the diagnosis covers a very wide range of abilities and behavioural features. Recently, much debate has centred on the nature of autism as a concept, and in particular the notion of an autistic spectrum (Wing, 1996). The term 'spectrum' is used to allow for wide variation in both the severity and the type of difficulties that fall within the triad of impairments. Indeed, many researchers now believe that a broader phenotype of autism may manifest itself as an unusual 'cognitive style' in close relations of people on the spectrum, and even in the general population at large.

Identifying the definitive features of autism and discovering how these may interact to produce such a variable overall picture is especially difficult because autism is accompanied by additional learning disabilities in as many as 70 per cent of cases (Boucher, 1996). Where the triad of impairments occurs in the presence of average or above average IQ, a description of either 'high-functioning' autism (HFA) or Asperger's syndrome (AS) may be applied. AS received a classification separate from autism for the first time in the most recent edition of the *Diagnostic and Statistical Manual of Mental Disorders* (DSM-IV, APA, 1994). Theoretically at least, AS is principally distinguished from autism by an absence of clinically significant childhood delays in language or general cognitive development. However in practice, differential diagnosis between AS and HFA may be open to subjective opinion, especially where insufficient information is available concerning early development. In short, the situation for diagnosticians and those trying to make use of diagnoses is complex to say the least.

Accepting the need to understand the diversity and complexity noted above, the majority of people with autism will need lifelong support of one kind or another. However, individuals with HFA or AS may learn ways of coping with the demands of everyday life that allow them both to live independently and to undertake study or employment successfully. Indeed, recent research suggests that autism may confer advantages in certain areas of psychological functioning, as well as disadvantages in others. As a result, people with autism may excel in particular areas whilst continuing to present with significant disabilities in areas described within the triad. There has even been speculation that a number of people at the pinnacle of their professions may have presented with the kind of 'single-mindedness' and social lack of interest that would today fulfil the criteria for autism or AS, Ludwig Wittgenstein and Albert Einstein being perhaps the most famous examples. Indeed, in our vignette that opens this chapter readers will note the successes of James (that are sometimes masked by his difficulties).

In some cases, people well into adulthood may become aware that they fit the diagnostic criteria for AS only after a lifetime of feeling alienated and baffled by the seemingly incomprehensible social conduct of those around them. The sometimes impressive social competence that individuals with HFA or AS may achieve will typically have been learnt through an unusually rule-based or 'reasoned' approach, in contrast to the more intuitive or 'natural feel' that most of us have for social interaction. Temple Grandin (in Sacks, 1995), a highly articulate woman with autism who holds a PhD, has described herself as 'an anthropologist on Mars' (Sacks, 1995: 248), using formulae based on observation to predict the otherwise unfathomable social conventions of 'the natives' (Sacks, 1995: 256). Marc Segar (1997), an energetic advocate for the rights of people with autism and AS, has even written 'A guide to coping, specifically for people with Asperger syndrome', which spells out rules on eye contact, appropriate behaviour at parties and so on, based on the assumption that 'autistic people have to understand scientifically what non-autistic people already understand instinctively' (Segar, 1997: 24). Inevitably, this kind of 'rule-based' approach to interaction results in somewhat inflexible strategies that work well in routine situations, but are potentially confounded by unfamiliar scenarios or events. The main aims of this chapter are to encourage ways of presenting information so that it 'makes sense' to people using this different kind of approach, and also to attempt to explain how it is that seemingly bizarre behaviours arise in autism.

Students with autism/AS in higher education

How many are there?

As far as the authors of this chapter are aware, no statistics are yet available regarding the numbers of students with HFA or AS in higher education. The dearth of research in this area may have arisen at least partly from the widespread (but mistaken) assumption that autism is likely to prohibit study at degree level and beyond. Fortunately, healthcare professionals are gradually becoming more aware of autism at the able end of the spectrum: indeed, the recent and dramatic increase reported in the incidence of autism may, in part, result from improved recognition at this level. Even so, it seems likely that a significant number of students may fit the criteria for autism or AS, without ever receiving an official diagnosis.

Identification of needs is, of course, the first stage to increasing accessibility to the higher education experience, both curricular and otherwise. Nonetheless, it should be emphasized that even students who have recognized their autism (through either official or self-diagnosis) may choose not to share this knowledge with staff or students at their place of study – often, for fear of misunderstanding and discrimination. By the age at which students typically enter higher education, most individuals with autism/AS will have developed a well-founded mistrust of others' interpretative abilities with regard to their diagnosis. It goes without saying that confidentiality should receive the utmost priority, over and above any perceived 'benefits' a member of teaching staff believes may ensue from passing on information regarding diagnosis. The issue of when and who to tell regarding diagnosis may be one better addressed via discussion between students with autism who have different experiences of disclosure, rather than through advice from professionals with no first-hand experience. (Possible avenues for joining such discussion are included in the resource section at the end of this chapter.)

The advantages arising from autism

Contemporary literature is increasingly coming around to the idea that autism may confer a different rather than merely a damaged way of thinking. For example, recent psychological research suggests that autism may be characterized by a heightened attention to detail that contrasts somewhat with the usual focusing on the gist or 'wider picture' (e.g. Frith and Happé, 1994). On the whole, it seems likely that this bias may be related to the tendency toward intense and narrow foci of interests and unusually good rote memory that often feature in autism and AS. Interestingly, autism also tends to be characterized by a strong bias toward the visual rather than verbal mode of information processing, though this in itself may be one area of difference between HFA and AS.

The strengths in autism combine with the triad of impairments to make some areas of endeavour generally more attractive and accessible to individuals on the spectrum than others. It is widely accepted by those involved in education and healthcare for people on the spectrum that autism appears with disproportionate frequency in families of certain professions – most notably, those related to engineering, science and information technology. Although research in this area has proved somewhat inconclusive, anecdotal evidence suggests that people on the spectrum may often have a natural affinity for computers, tasks involving facts and figures (as in mathematics and the sciences), and visually based skills such as those involved in technical drawing. In a very general sense, then, it may be that these aptitudes tend to be reflected in students' choice of courses, with an increased incidence in associated areas of study. This is not to say, of course, that students on the spectrum are exempt from any programme of study – here, as elsewhere in matters related to autism, one does not have to look far to find exceptions to the rule.

Most interesting of all, perhaps, is the possibility that academia might be attractive to individuals on the spectrum in and of itself. On a Web site dedicated to 'University students with autism and Asperger's syndrome', Sainsbury (2001) suggests that, in many ways, university life and autism may be eminently suited. Anyone who works in higher education will be familiar with members of academic staff who seem more at home among their books than in the company of people. As Sainsbury notes, it may be that the stereotype of the 'absent-minded professor' is itself a tell-tale sign of the prevalence of (undiagnosed) AS at work in higher education. Certainly, the high levels of tolerance for people who don't 'fit in' (with society at large) that may be seen to permeate the higher education ethos is a feature of university life that many students with HFA or AS find attractive.

The particular strengths that characterize autism mean that, given the appropriate support, students on the spectrum may well excel in their chosen field. Indeed, as one student with AS recently pointed out, individuals on the spectrum may need to be especially gifted if they are to overcome the non-academic difficulties at primary and secondary levels in order to gain access to university in the first place! Furthermore, such natural aptitude may be further enabled by the difficulties with, and/or lack of interest in, social mores that typify autism and AS. Given the relative absence of socially based distractions, students on the spectrum may well be more apt at spending their time studying than would be the case with their fellow students.

Strategies for access and inclusion

Diversity of needs

The following subsections offer a broad overview of the kinds of problems that students on the spectrum may experience as they progress from application to an institution of higher education through to eventual graduation. Once again, it is essential to stress the diversity of needs that characterize this particular student population. The present chapter can only give the reader a general impression of areas which may prove problematic, principally in order to raise awareness of the pervasive nature of differences associated with AS or HFA. What we can by no means do is offer a 'one size fits all' description of ideal provision. Not only will needs vary enormously between individuals, but there may also be fluctuations in sensory and attentional circumstances that make performance by the same student somewhat erratic over time. Even the most capable student may experience temporary 'meltdown' given just the wrong set of environmental factors. Awareness of this possibility may go a long way to explaining otherwise puzzling inconsistencies in the performance of a given student.

A student with AS who responded to an early draft of this chapter expressed his personal view of the primary difficulties he faces and the subsequent need for tutors to interpret carefully the roots of his difficulties:

> Although autism is generally seen as a disorder that is primarily social in nature, most of those social deficits are based on sensory problems and on cognitive difficulties that arise from those. I think it would help if teachers were told that it might clarify a lot if they thought of us as people with hearing, vision and tactile problems. It may make it easier for them to understand what our problems are. I've seen that as soon as you mention the A-

word, people get stuck in all kinds of silly beliefs about the nature of autism and cannot move past those prejudices, because they have nothing concrete to replace them with. Saying that I have AS clarifies nothing for most people. Saying that I suffer from prosopagnosia, CAPD, scotopic sensitivity disorder, synesthesia and a general incapacity to process visual information leads to much more understanding.

We need to stress here that the above is a personal account of the difficulties faced. We suggest that tutors need to accept that needs will be likely to vary from one individual to another, and it follows therefore that there can be no substitute for asking the individual how best his or her needs may be met. In fact, it is not uncommon for people with AS/HFA to offer written advice, either self-authored or written by a healthcare professional well known to them, concerning the kinds of difficulties that may be encountered and how best these might be dealt with (an example of an 'accommodations letter' of this kind can be found via a link from the 'University students with autism and Asperger's syndrome' Web site referred to earlier). Generally speaking, then, it is anticipated that the disability officer at an institution of higher education will work in partnership with a given student and relevant staff to best meet needs as these arise. Where a student does not seem to know how best he or she might be helped, and with the student's full consent, it may be appropriate to seek professional advice. Currently Prospects, the adult service provided by the National Autistic Society, offers a limited outreach service to institutions of higher education, and there are hopes of extending this in the future.

Although of course a generalization, it might be added here that people on the spectrum tend to be less likely than others to use deceitful means in order to exploit a system or situation. It is common for individuals with HFA/AS of all ages to be taken advantage of by less scrupulous people, often because of difficulties with understanding that apparently good or kind behaviour may be driven by bad intentions. Indeed, the less attractive facets of human intelligence are often among those most mysterious to people on the spectrum. However, this need not necessarily be the case – one of the students who commented on an earlier draft of this chapter noted a contrary, though equally problematic, position:

We do get the general idea that people mostly do not have our best interests at heart. Since we have little capacity to distinguish between good and bad intentions, quite a few of us become quite paranoid, especially when in distress, and may complain of complots and other seemingly delusional ideas.

It would be a good idea to stress that one should not make the mistake of jumping to the conclusion that those people are perhaps paranoid schizophrenics. Being paranoid makes good sense if you have AS or HFA and has nothing to do with schizophrenia.

Clearly the situation may be complicated, but as a general rule we would suggest that it may be safer than usual to treat a request for special allowance as a genuine reflection of need, rather than as an attempt to gain advantage over fellow students.

Of course, in many cases, an institution of HE may not have knowledge of diagnosis prior to accepting a student onto a course. Nonetheless, in meeting appropriate standards of quality, there is currently an expectation that institutions will offer a provision that is 'sufficiently flexible to cater to individuals' changing needs throughout their periods of study' (QAA, 1999). Indeed, the present chapter is as much concerned with helping staff to identify profiles of needs that seem consistent with autism or AS, as it is with meeting the needs of those students who have declared an official diagnosis. The experience and knowledge of those people who are aware of their diagnosis is likely to act as a far better guide to meeting needs than the rather cursory information contained here. On the other hand, recognizing that a given student shows a cluster of related needs may be helpful without the need to establish a diagnostic 'label'.

Gaining access to HE

If one aims to increase accessibility to HE in the most immediate sense, then one must include some reference to the process by which students come to enter university in the first place. It seems likely that many would-be students with AS/HFA never receive the opportunity for tertiary education because of anxiety related to perceptions of college life or problems encountered during application.

Of the application procedures typically required of new entrants, it seems probable that the interview will prove most problematic for prospective students with AS/HFA. Whilst most students will experience nervousness prior to an interview for placement at university, this is likely to be in an altogether different category to the severe anxiety that may afflict an applicant on the spectrum. Anxiety of this kind may be reduced substantially by proactive organization of the day's proceedings, such that the timings, locations and (to some degree) likely procedures are made clear in advance – and whenever possible, adhered to. A simple map showing relevant venues, or (better still) an arrow system on corridor walls, may go a long way to reducing the confusion and associated stress induced by unfamiliar surroundings.

Whatever the institution's general policy, it may be that an applicant on the spectrum should be given the option of being accompanied in the interview by a person of his or her choice. Regardless of whether this person is an informal or professional advocate, it may be helpful to establish the role he/she is to play prior to the day of interview. While it may be enough for this second person simply to 'be there' for the applicant, a degree of mediation may be perfectly appropriate, especially where communication is concerned. The social and communication difficulties associated with autism and AS combine to make a range of spoken and non-verbal aspects of interaction problematic, especially where the non-autistic conversant is unfamiliar with either the individual or with autism in general. In managing the interview, perhaps the most important rule of thumb is to be explicit. Everyday interaction – both formal and informal – is governed by a multitude of implicit rules that we typically take for granted. Information communicated by eye gaze, gesture and body language, not to mention intonation and timing of speech, help the non-autistic among us to successfully read 'deeper' meanings not contained within the literal sense of the words we hear. Autism and AS confer a specific disadvantage in reading meanings of these kinds. Consequently, where a given question receives an unexpected response, be prepared to give more explicit prompts regarding the kind of information that you wanted to elicit.

The same 'breakdown' between speaker and listener may be equally evident when the roles are reversed. Individuals with autism, and especially AS, may present with highly fluent and articulate language skills that lack a corresponding level of conversational competence. Areas of particular difficulty include the appropriate continuation of a given topic, a picking up of cues related to conversational turn-taking, and the ability to communicate necessary and/or sufficient information appropriate for a given listener. Added to this, the speech of many individuals on the spectrum may feature unusual pitch or pace, while eye contact, gesture and body language may seem 'not quite right' given the social and communicative contexts involved. These atypicalities are far from superficial. On the contrary, they are representative of the complex difficulties with social meaning that lie at the heart of autism and AS.

Settling into HE

Orientation

Assuming that potential obstacles at the application stage are avoided, students with HFA/AS will be faced with the difficult task of finding their way around university life. At the most immediate level, this will mean orienting themselves on the campus in order to find rooms where they have a lecture or seminar. Many individuals on the spectrum experience significant problems with organizing landmarks into a 'mental map' in order to find their way around. Once again, clear and consistent signposting and diagrams may be of value in helping students reach their destinations on time. This whole issue of orientation is of course a significant one for many new students and staff – what needs to be recognized here is that in autism the problems are significantly greater, and the subsequent level of emotional upset potentially far greater.

University facilities

Problems with finding one's way around continue on a smaller scale with orienting oneself around university facilities such as the library, canteen and launderette. Many students with HFA/AS report being somewhat overwhelmed by the size and complexity of university libraries (as noted in the vignette that opened this chapter). Where this is a problem, and the student in question is amenable, it may be helpful if library staff are given some introduction to the student's specific needs so that they will be on hand to help over the course of study. This example highlights the possibility that people who come into contact with a student in limited capacities might be made aware of specific needs rather than informed of the diagnosis as a whole. Some students (such as the student quoted earlier) may feel more comfortable with telling people that they have specific difficulties with, for example, recognizing faces (prosopagnosia), or with hearing what is said when there is a lot of background noise, than with going through the rather more arduous process of explaining these characteristics within the context of their diagnosis. This option seems a sensible compromise that enables needs to be better met while preserving confidentiality where the student favours this.

An alternative or additional approach might be to have a fellow student on hand to accompany the student with HFA/AS when he or she is familiarizing him/herself with facilities at the beginning of term. 'Buddy' systems of this kind have been found to be successful to a point, although care needs to be taken in monitoring that both parties are comfortable with the way the arrangement is working out.

Coping with the curriculum

Lectures and seminars

Academic progress is one area where sharing information related to needs really should be able to make a positive difference. A range of factors that could be easily improved often impedes students who might otherwise be highly successful. Regrettably, however, remediative measures may often be forced to take the form of 'damage limitation' rather than of tackling the root cause in a way that creates a truly 'autism-friendly' learning environment. A good example here concerns perhaps the single most frequent complaint offered by students on the spectrum with regard to accessibility of any public space – namely, the damaging effects of the ubiquitous fluorescent light bulb. The sensory differences commonly associated with autism and AS make the flickering illumination available in most venues highly detrimental to students' abilities to attend to and follow proceedings. Yet, given the still pervasive belief that 'disability occurs within the individual', a comprehensive change of lighting in public buildings may not be a realistic expectation. As a result, a poor second best solution may have to confine itself to offering students the choice of where to sit in a given teaching space, so that distraction is limited to some extent. This then would be seen as a low-level pragmatic solution.

Seating position may be an issue for reasons other than lighting. Depending on the medium of lecture presentation and general noise levels, it may be that a seat near to the lecturer is required. An aisle seat will almost always be preferable due to the discomfort experienced by most individuals on the spectrum when in close proximity to unfamiliar people. It may be that an understanding needs to be established among teaching staff and fellow students that some movement between different seating positions is likely to be necessary during a lengthy presentation. This is because fluctuations in either environmental (such as light, noise, smell) or sensory processing factors may mean a previously advantageous position becomes less so.

Hypersensitivity to smell, touch and sound may combine with the social and communication difficulties experienced by many people on the spectrum to make working in groups among the most problematic aspects of in-class education. Such hypersensitivity (and sometimes hyposensitivity) may be variable over time, and in some individuals may relate to periods of illness. In extreme cases, and where the exercise in question allows, these factors may warrant an alternative (and more solitary) approach to a given task.

Modern methods of teaching have already gone some way to improving access for students on the spectrum. Although, as always, preference will vary between individuals, there seems to be a general leaning in autism towards computer-based media over other forms of presentation – especially when this is contrasted with a more social, group-based approach. Many students with HFA/AS will prefer to use a computer when note taking, and, ideally (as is often the case nowadays), the lecture will be accessible on the Web for students to download and refer to on-screen in class. Where the facilities to present material online are not available, it may be highly advantageous to give students on the spectrum prior access to clear handouts which offer a comprehensive inclusion of key information presented in the lecture as a whole.

When confronted with a large amount of information for the first time, students with HFA/AS may well have difficulty separating those parts of a presentation that they are required to attend to from those intended to be merely anecdotal or humorous asides. Once again, the golden rule of 'be explicit' can be applied liberally, and key parts of a presentation should be highlighted by a suitable means of emphasis, verbal and/or otherwise. Just as importantly, where the lecturer wishes students to recognize associations or contrasts between information presented, or between information and experience, this should be made explicit. In some cases, it may be appropriate for students to record a lecture (using either audio or video equipment) so that they can review information in a distraction-free environment.

Many people on the spectrum find it difficult to infer the meaning that is intended by someone using non-literal speech acts – for example, those containing metaphor or irony. Wherever possible, then, it may be helpful if figurative language and indirect allusion can be avoided in favour of a more direct style of presentation. Over-literal interpretation of language is perhaps the clearest example of how people with HFA/AS may simply 'miss' a meaning of consensus, because they are applying a somewhat alternative and – to some extent – more 'logical' approach to that employed by others. An unusual approach to meaning-making often extends beyond language in autism/AS to include idiosyncratic interpretations of situations, events, ideas and even objects. While there will be a consistency to this which has both rhyme and reason to the individual in question, the 'misunderstandings' that arise may often appear quite bizarre to those around. As a result, it is important that individual tutorial time is offered to students on the spectrum in order to monitor their understanding of important information communicated during class. A question and answer routine will quickly establish whether information has been integrated by the student into his/her wider understanding in the way the lecturer intended. Where this has not been the case, the problem may well be rectifiable through an alternative approach, that works through what needs to be understood in a more structured and logical fashion.

Coursework

Ensuring that students have an accurate understanding is especially important when it comes to elucidating coursework requirements. Coursework is an area of potential strength for students on the spectrum, because they can work at their own pace using preferred methods. However, care needs to be taken to ensure that students have understood what is required of them. Providing students with the opportunity to check that they have understood the demands made by a given assignment may do much to relieve confusion and related anxiety. Moreover, many people with HFA/AS may have difficulty with planning their time, and with organizing their approach to work that involves a number of different elements. Where this is the case, it may be appropriate to discuss targets for discrete sections of a project, working toward completion of the assignment as a whole.

Exams

Many students with HFA/AS contrast their good performance on coursework over an academic year with the poor marks they receive for examinations. Problematic aspects of exams singled out for special mention include the time restriction imposed on thinking and writing, the requirement that students use a pen rather than a computer, the close proximity of examinees, and the ambiguity of many exam questions. While these factors may affect performance in any student to some degree, the differences inherent in HFA/AS may mean that students on the spectrum are simply not competing on a 'level playing field' given standard exam arrangements. For example, students with HFA/AS may actually be physically slower and clumsier in their writing skills. They will be far more likely to experience unacceptable levels of anxiety, with atypical and highly detrimental effects on the capacity for remembering and reasoning.

These problems are easily remedied by the provision of a separate room in which to sit exams (preferably one without fluorescent lighting), the use

172 Specific learning issues

of a computer to write on, and (where needed) additional time to complete in. Ideally, a member of staff should also be on hand at the beginning of the exam to establish that the student has interpreted the exam question correctly. Clearly, on this latter point, the regulations of the particular university would need to be taken into account.

Extracurricular campus life

Outside the academic side of university life, there may be more pernicious factors at play that are not as easily addressed by practical means as those outlined above. The incidence of depression may well be higher in students on the spectrum than in general, often because of the overwhelming stress induced by the social pressures of communal living. Students with HFA/AS differ radically in their attitudes towards the difficulty with 'fitting in' that unites all people on the spectrum. Some are happy simply avoiding social situations that, in any event, hold no interest for them. Where this is the case, it would be entirely inappropriate for a campus counsellor to probe for deep-seated emotional problems that just are not there (a not unheard-of experience!). At the other extreme, however, are those who never come to terms with involuntary isolation, and make repeated and failed attempts to make friends, often feeling exploited and/or rejected in the process. Although no statistics are available on the subject, it seems likely to us that it will be these students who are most vulnerable to mental illness. (It may be worth noting here that people with AS are often not very facially expressive, and that depression in a person who is generally somewhat flat and expressionless may easily be missed.) Between these two extremes lie the majority of students on the spectrum, who may experience a degree of anguish as a result of unpleasant or confusing social encounters, but also tend to be less socially motivated than the average student and more content to spend at least some time alone.

Clearly, time at university is one in which many people explore the making of commitments to sexual partners. The difficulties faced in this respect are perhaps best summed up by one of the young people with AS who responded to an early draft of this chapter:

> We, like retarded people, are not supposed to have sex, but I am afraid this is wishful thinking. … Quite a lot of people on the spectrum are late bloomers in this respect and may not be interested in this part of social intercourse at all. … Other people are actually quite desperate to also get a girl or boyfriend, and will feel increasingly different because they lack experience in this field.

Providing support to students in these circumstances is difficult, not least because of the reliance on their coming to ask for help. As with any student group, the more severe the problem, the less likely it may be that individuals will feel able to approach staff for support. It may be that a sudden drop in academic progress acts as a warning that all is not well, or that other students complain of, or are even openly antagonistic toward, the student in question. In such instances, it may be appropriate for staff to intervene, provided great care is taken, or to offer possible avenues for addressing a given problem. In some cases, it may be that a practical solution can be offered. For example, escalating antipathy between room-mates because of 'anti-social' or 'eccentric' behaviour on the part of a student with HFA/AS might be remedied by the offer of a single room. Equally, it may be that a given student is perplexed and anxious about a specific social encounter that might easily be explained by someone who is sensitive to a case of misinterpretation. Whether these issues are best addressed by a tutor or other professional must remain a matter for discretion given the individual circumstances. It may be worth noting that counselling has been found to be useful by some people on the spectrum in certain circumstances, although previous and widespread inappropriate use of this resource with this population urges caution against an uninformed prescription of therapy. Where a given student seeks counselling, it is advisable that the professional acquaints him/herself with the nature of HFA/AS before 'jumping in at the deep end' with therapy too eagerly.

It should also be emphasized that many students on the spectrum take an active role in extracurricular activities such as sports and clubs, where they may show high levels of competence and commitment. Where a given student has a specific aptitude that he or she would like to express through these avenues, support may be needed to ensure that accessibility to such extracurricular activities is not compromised by socially related problems.

Making the transition from HE to the workplace

Many curricula these days include some preparation for the workplace. This may take the form of work placements during the programme of education, of training in standard application and interview procedures at the end of the final year, or a combination of both. Where work experience is included, it may be that extra care needs to be taken in monitoring progress. Where appropriate, a personal tutor who has become familiar with the individual student might be on hand to act either as a mediator/

troubleshooter should the need arise, or as a resource for the student to 'sound out' on perceived problems or concerns.

Where this is handled in the right way, training for applications and interviews may be invaluable to students on the spectrum. Use of video has been found to be particularly effective for teaching social skills to primary and secondary school age students with autism. This approach provides learners with feedback regarding their performance that can be discussed with a view to offering concrete ways of improving specific skills. It may be necessary to provide a given student with set rules for approaching an interview situation, with quite detailed advice on eye contact and body language. Prospects, mentioned earlier in the chapter, specializes in supporting adults with HFA/AS through employment, and may be a useful source of advice on how best to help individuals with their interview skills.

Summary

In this chapter, we have tried to offer a brief introduction to autism and Asperger's syndrome, together with a general outline of some of the ways in which access to HE might be restricted for students with related special needs. Throughout the chapter, we have emphasized the likely breadth and diversity of needs that this student population may present with, and encouraged staff to refer to the individual in all cases. In offering general guiding principles aimed at increasing accessibility for students on the spectrum, we highlighted the need to be explicit, and the practice of monitoring progress in both curricular and extracurricular areas.

Acknowledgements

The authors would like to thank Claire Sainsbury and members of the University Students with Autism and Asperger's syndrome mailing list (http://www.users.dircon.co.uk/~cns/list.html) for the helpful advice they have offered regarding the content of this chapter. Also we would like to acknowledge the help given by many students with autism and AS and their parents in formulating this chapter; in particular we would like to acknowledge the insightful and thought-provoking comments of Darius and Natalie.

Resources

An impressive list of resources for students with disabilities of any kind, and for people with autism or Asperger's syndrome in particular, can be found at http://www.users.dircon.co.uk/~cns/index.html (Sainsbury, 2001).

Prospects
Studio 8, The Ivories, 6 Northampton St
London N1 2HY
Tel: 0207 7047450
http://www.oneworld.org/autism-uk/nas/prospect.html

References

American Psychiatric Association (APA) (1994) *Diagnostic and Statistical Manual of Mental Disorders*, 4th edn, American Psychiatric Association, Washington DC

Boucher, J (1996) What could possibly explain autism? in *Theories of Theories of Mind*, ed P Carruthers and P K Smith, pp 223–41, Cambridge University Press, Cambridge

Frith, U and Happé, F (1994) Autism: beyond 'theory of mind', *Cognition*, **50**, pp 115–32

Quality Assurance Agency for Higher Education (QAAHE) (1999) Code of Practice for the Assurance of Academic Quality and Standards in Higher Education, Section 3: Students with Disabilities, QAAHE, Gloucester

Rutter, M and Schopler, E (1987) Autism and pervasive developmental disorders: conceptual and diagnostic issues, *Journal of Autism and Developmental Disorders*, **17**, pp 159–86

Sacks, O (1995) *An Anthropologist on Mars*, Picador, London

Sainsbury, C (2001) University students with autism and Asperger's syndrome [Online] http://www.users.dircon.co.uk/~cns/index.html

Segar, M (1997) *A Guide to Coping, Specifically for People with Asperger syndrome*, unpublished paper

Wing, L (1996) *The Autistic Spectrum: A guide for parents and professionals*, Constable, London

Wing, L and Gould, J (1979) Severe impairments of social interaction and associated abnormalities in children: epidemiology and classification, *Journal of Autism and Developmental Disorders*, **9**, pp 11–29

Further reading

Attwood, T (1997) *Asperger's syndrome: A guide for parents and professionals*, Jessica Kingsley, London

Jordan, R R (1999) *Autistic Spectrum Disorders: An introductory handbook for practitioners*, David Fulton, London

Lawson, W (1998) Family and personal section: my life as an exchange student with Asperger syndrome on an exchange programme from Monash University, Australia, to the University of Bradford, England, *Autism*, **2** (3), pp 290–95

11

Issues for pedagogy (2)

Stuart Powell

Diagnosis

Luckett and Powell note first that the diagnosis of autism covers a wide range of abilities and behavioural features, and second that the knowledge that an individual has a diagnosis of autism only guides the lecturer so far in understanding that individual. Similarly, Cottrell points out that 'dyslexia' is something of a misnomer in that it does not accurately describe the difficulties concerned. As noted in Issues for pedagogy (1), it is all the other factors that are brought together with the 'condition' that add up to the set of individual learning characteristics with which the student approaches the teaching and learning situation.

Luckett and Powell also draw attention to the fact that mention of the diagnosis may provoke forms of prejudicial reaction. The quote from the student illustrates this: 'as soon as you mention the A-word, people get stuck in all kinds of silly beliefs about the nature of autism and cannot move past those prejudices'. That particular student's response was to redefine his condition in terms that he felt would be more helpful to his tutors. Others may choose to give specific examples of areas of difficulty (such as recognizing faces) rather than rely on a global diagnosis to convey the meaning they perceive is necessary to their tutors. The general issue arising is that university lecturers should treat diagnoses not as labels giving clear instructions as to how to proceed, but rather as signposts that indicate a direction. The exact path that is followed in relation to that direction is one that may be influenced by a more colloquial description of learning features negotiated with the student and understandable in terms of the real constraints and possibilities of the classroom. It may well be that, through a process of negotiation between student and tutor, a simplified and individualized set of guidelines (for effective learning for the particular student) can be developed and circulated to all lecturers that the student is likely to encounter.

Importance of the individual's history

This issue was mentioned in Issues for pedagogy (1), but is perhaps worth repeating here, because the example given by Parke adds to one's appreciation that what is needed is not only knowledge of the fact that, in this case, the student has English as a second language, but also how that student came to acquire that second language. Parke draws an important distinction between learning that occurred in 'naturalistic' as opposed to 'tutored' settings. He argues that the one position is in many significant ways the reverse of the other, and also that students will emerge from one kind of learning to another. It is clearly important therefore for tutors to have some understanding of background as well as basic facts.

Again, it would be inappropriate for educators to operate on the basis of a label ('for this particular student, English is a second language') without trying to understand and take into account how that student has learnt what he or she has learnt. The process of learning that has gone on is as important in many ways as the state of students' knowledge and skills, in this case of the English language, that they bring at the outset of their university life. Similarly, with autism it is important to know what kind of learning experiences the individual has had if an appropriate approach at university is to be attained. To give a specific example: if an individual with autism has learnt certain ways of behaving in social settings by carrying written prompts in her Filofax (a strategy used by several individuals within my own experience) then to deny her such notes would be potentially disastrous. In short, devising a teaching approach to enable social integration by a judgement based on the individual's behaviour alone would be wholly inappropriate when that person's means of attaining that behaviour, and the historical route by which he or she arrived at his/her present level of skill are unknown.

Cottrell's description of the progress of Selima through her years before university illustrates powerfully the emotional impact that her dyslexia had upon her. University lecturers need to recognize that there may well be emotional issues around the student's approach to learning that are not directly related to the condition itself but that are nonetheless pervasive and deep rooted. Again, an understanding of Selima's history would help to explain her present situation.

Cultural background

Clearly the cultural background of the student is a part of his/her personal history. I separate it out from the above section, however, simply to draw attention to the weight of expectations that both teachers and students may bring to the learning environment. Parke, in his section, 'Roles in the class-room', takes the example of students from China to illustrate contrasting expectations of the learning process. When discussing individuals within the range of different approaches to learning that are cited in this book, it is important to bear in mind therefore the cultural background that has formed the way in which individuals learn, and in particular, perhaps, the expectations that they bring with them. Enculturation may be seen as a factor influencing development largely independently of any disability or specific learning difficulty, though clearly different cultures respond differently to different disabilities and difficulties, so the 'independence' here can never be total.

In terms of the relationship between culture and overall development, the exception to the above may be those individuals with autism described by Luckett and Powell. For them learning may be best described as acul-tural, and they may seem to have developed almost immune from cultural influences. I would suggest that of all students considered in this book, those with autism are unique in this particular feature of their development.

Advantages as well as disadvantages

As noted elsewhere in this book, it is all too easy to adopt a deficit model when engaging with a student with declared special learning needs. Luckett and Powell point out, however, that some of the features of autism confer advantages on the individual in certain areas of life – notably some aspects of academia. They note the single-mindedness, ability to concentrate (to what may seem an obsessive extent), heightened attention to detail, unusually good rote memory, ability to process visual information and social lack of interest (leading to few if any social distractions) that typify some students with autism. They also point out, using their vignette, that some of the difficulties, or at least lecturers' perceptions of those difficulties, may mask the student's learning advantages.

Cottrell makes a similar point in relation to students with dyslexia. Individuals with dyslexia may present as having difficulty with learning, but they may in reality find some higher order tasks easier than certain lower order ones. As she notes, individuals with dyslexia prefer tasks involving 'deep understanding' to those involving rote learning, and in this sense some aspects of university life may suit them better than the schooling they underwent. It is important therefore for lecturers to analyse with some care the whole of the profile of the student as learner, including his/her skills and abilities as well as difficulties. There may well be occasions where students can be enabled to maximize the usefulness of their strengths. Again, as noted in Issues for pedagogy (1), the individual will come to the university setting with a record of educational successes, as well as challenges met. It may be worthwhile to examine those successes – what the student has achieved – and learn from the processes and procedures that led to them.

'Time is the key'

Cottrell points out that being dyslexic does not necessarily mean that an individual cannot do something. Rather it means that they may need encouragement, specific means and, above all, time in order to achieve their potential. Individuals with dyslexia can perform well on tasks where they work at their own pace, but will fail when those same tasks are undertaken under timed conditions. Cottrell cites research suggesting that children with dyslexia take 10 times as long to learn certain sub-skills as their non-dyslexic peers. Those with autism as described by Luckett and Powell often need longer to assimilate just what is being asked of them than do their peers of similar ability: they may need to work out in a mechanistic way what the intentions of the lecturer are, where their peers 'just know' what is intended. Similarly, the students Parke discusses for whom English is a second language need to overcome any uncertainties about the language of the task before they can deal with the task itself. Positive discrimination in terms of time on task may therefore be needed, to enable all these students to gain the success of which they are capable.

Disclosure

Students may choose not to disclose their diagnosis, or may ask for confidentiality from their tutors. Cottrell describes a case study in which Selima decides to hide her dyslexia so as to avoid the rejection she fears, basing this course of action on her previous experiences of education. Luckett and Powell indicate their view that confidentiality must be given priority. Issues of the benefits that may arise from disclosure, for example that structured help of an appropriate kind can be given by a wider range of lecturers and by peers, need to be weighed against the student's rights of confidentiality. The way forward must involve open discussion with the student, of a kind that can only exist within relationships where there is mutual trust. An issue for educators, then, is to find ways of establishing and maintaining trust so that the benefits and disadvantages of disclosure can be explored fully and realistically. Again, openness to all possibilities and a fundamentally honest approach (including for example about one's own uncertainties as a tutor) is required.

The interview process

Luckett and Powell discuss the interview process from the perspective of students with autistic spectrum disorders (ASD). They note in particular the need for explicitness and for understanding of the way in which those with ASD may respond in the interview situation. In general, the interview is the opportunity for the tone of subsequent relations to be set. The kind of mutual openness that is argued for throughout this book needs to be established at this stage, if the sense of mutual trust, which I have argued for as of real significance in the development of successful learning situations for the student, is to be achieved. The interview is a significant opportunity to set out by the tutor what is known and what is not known about a particular diagnosis and about a particular course of study. Similarly, it is the opportunity for students to discuss their own perceptions of their learning needs – what they aspire to achieve and how best they think that can be done.

Assumptions about language use

Parke illustrates that in the English language words that at one level are closely connected and have a meaningful 'core' (he cites photo, photograph, photographer, photographic, photographically) may, when spoken aloud, have only occasional similarities. For all three types of learner discussed in this part of the book (and indeed for those learners with a hearing impairment mentioned earlier), difficulties can arise when tutors are unaware of the ever-changing nature of language according to context and usage. The learner who has only an emerging grasp of the complexities of language is vulnerable when a tutor uses language without taking full account of their situation.

For individuals with autism, as discussed by Powell and Luckett, language is hard for the learner to produce and receive precisely because it is flexible and lacks rigidity: the meaning of words shifts with context, intonation and intention. Variations as described above in the case of 'photograph' and the use of language in a less than straightforward way (as in homonyms, homophones, irony and metaphor) may be a part of academic life at one level, but may disadvantage some learners at another. This is not to argue that lecturers should not use metaphor, for example, but that they need to recognize that such usage will be received by the 'audience' of students at very different levels and to very different effects. What may help understanding for some will hinder it in others. What is clearly necessary, then, is a balanced approach to use of language: an avoidance of assumptions that meaning will be clear as a result of particular kinds of usage, and a use of alternative explanations and perhaps modes of delivery in order to accommodate the range of individual learning needs in relation to how best to access meaning via language.

Part five

Mental health issues

12

Students with schizophrenia in higher education

James Wade

Introduction

For many, the term 'schizophrenia' conjures images of someone with a 'split personality'. Further, shocking news headlines sometimes serve to reinforce negative stereotypes and misunderstandings about severe mental illness. It is important to stress here that schizophrenia is an illness that can be very debilitating and often strikes young people during the late teens and early 20s.

One in 100 people (1 per cent of the population) will experience schizophrenia before the age of 45. Students with a diagnosis of schizophrenia can succeed at their studies and, similarly to students with other disabilities, may require assistance to make their studying a successful experience.

This chapter opens with a vignette, and subsequently offers a basic introduction to the illness, its stigma, potential obstacles faced by students, coursework flexibility, and the importance of understanding that we all have mental health, as well as emphasizing the role universities can play in promoting mental health awareness and tackling discrimination. The chapter is not meant as a 'crisis' guide.

Before we get into the chapter proper I would like to introduce a vignette. The vignette is based on an actual situation that arose while I was working for the Rethink: Severe Mental Illness 'Advice Service' (formerly NSF, the National Schizophrenia Fellowship) as part of a student awareness-raising project. The names of individuals and the university have been omitted, as the vignette is not intended as a name and shame exercise, more an overview of what can happen when communications break down.

Vignette

The switchboard operator at the Rethink office asked me to speak with a woman who was insistent we help her. I was informed the woman was agitated and would only speak to me, the student project worker. I took the call and listened patiently. The woman had a son, now in his mid-20s. He had attended a UK university and reached his third year final exams where he experienced a psychosis. Because of the intensity and length of the 'episode' the young man was unable to complete his final exams.

The university lost contact with the young man. Meanwhile the young man experienced a long period of unwellness followed by a period of re-adjustment to his illness. During this time, the young man's mother had had to overcome many obstacles, understanding her son's condition, prognosis, and likely implications for her family. Approximately two and a half years after the initial episode, the young man's mother was trying to help her son rebuild his life. Speaking with a personal friend, the mother learnt about aegrotat degrees. An aegrotat degree is a discretionary status awarded by universities to students who have been unable to complete their studies due to exceptional circumstances.

Her son had attended university regularly and achieved consistently good grades. With this in mind the mother corresponded with the university to enquire about the possibility of awarding her son an aegrotat degree. Her son was still too unwell to use his degree for employment purposes, but if he was successful with the request, she thought that at least he would gain the recognition of achievement for his student work. The mother phoned and wrote to the university on numerous occasions. Despite reminders from the mother, the university failed to prioritize the enquiry. Eventually, the mother was so distraught with her lack of progress that she phoned a national radio station with her story, and then immediately phoned the National Schizophrenia Fellowship to explain what she planned to do and ask our advice.

The phone call to me from the mother occurred at the beginning of the academic year, just as students were beginning and resuming their studies.

As you can imagine, this was a newsworthy story for a national radio station. It was also a potential public relations disaster for the university. With the mother's permission, I phoned a contact in counselling services at the university and explained the delicate situation. Fortunately, the university telephoned the mother immediately, the potential public relations disaster was avoided, and eventually the young man was awarded an aegrotat degree in recognition of his university achievement.

Vignette observations

The vignette described above serves to illustrate that severe mental illness strikes young people at any time. The illness does not differentiate by class, creed or colour, nor is it preceded by clear signs. The young man in the vignette had not shown a predisposition to mental illness while studying, and it was only during the final year exams that he experienced psychosis. These difficulties rarely if ever present in neat parcels, and it is unfortunate the university did not manage to remain in contact with the young man and his family. One such consideration is where the young person is treated, for example away from the university location. (I do not know whether the young man described above was treated near the university or closer to his family home.) The aegrotat degree enquiry was made worse by the mother's inability to make progress despite telephone calls and registered letters to the university.

As a result of the above, the university thoroughly reviewed its policy about mental health and illness, as well as its procedures for replying to requests for information. The vignette helps us to understand that the young man was affected at a crucial stage of studying, and poor follow-up allowed him to 'slip through the net'.

Early intervention

The importance of early intervention to long-term outcome of severe mental illness for individuals is becoming more apparent. The government has prioritized the rollout of approximately 50 Early Intervention Services UK nationwide from April 2002, aimed at helping adolescents. These services aim to engage with young people in the early stages of psychosis to limit the impact of the illness through a combination of medication and community support.

Rethink is working with IRIS, Initiative to Reduce the Impact of Schizophrenia, a West Midlands-based group of mental health professionals, to develop further understanding of early intervention and develop practical ways of implementing it . Contact details for IRIS can be found at the end of this chapter.

Severe mental illness

The following extract from the Rethink *Students and Mental Health Resource Pack* (1995) gives a basic introduction to severe mental illness:

> This term usually refers to mental health problems which seriously disrupt a person's capacity to function in their everyday life and may endanger their own safety and those of others. Perhaps it is useful to think of mental health as a continuum ranging from the relatively mild anxieties, disappointments and frustrations of everyday life to severe problems affecting mood, the ability to think and communicate rationally, and even sensory perception. In an extreme case of mental disorder an individual may be psychotic and lose touch with reality to the extent of hearing and seeing things which are not there, and holding delusional beliefs. An individual can experience a psychosis due to a number of reasons but for most it will be part of a severe mental illness such as schizophrenia or manic depression.
>
> (Rethink, 1995: 6)

Symptoms

There is a range of symptoms associated with schizophrenia, and each person will be affected differently. Individuals may develop false beliefs, have hallucinations, be deflated in mood, experience behavioural changes, their thought processes may become confused and subsequently their speech jumbled. These symptoms may be summarized as follows:

- **False beliefs** often manifest as others conspiring against the person, or belief that the person is someone else, often a famous person.
- **Hallucinations** include hearing voices. A person may be able to 'hear' several voices as well as smell, taste, feel or see things that others without the illness cannot see.
- **Mood** may be deflated. The person may feel lethargic and unresponsive to previously positive stimuli such as friends and interests.

- **Behaviour** can change, and the person may feel isolated and become socially withdrawn.
- **Thinking** may be confused and speech jumbled.

Nobody knows whether they have a predisposition to a mental illness. Entering university is an exciting time for most if not all students, but it is not without the stresses and strains associated with living away from home and adjusting to living independently, as well as managing new and often competing demands. Most people experience ups and downs in their everyday life, and develop ways to alleviate feelings of sadness and deal with the kinds of setbacks that are an inevitable part of daily living. Clearly universities set out to offer challenge, and an inevitable part of that challenge is the possibility of disappointment and even distress. Unfortunately some people cope less well, and their difficulties can develop into mental illness.

This chapter is perhaps not the appropriate place to discuss in detail ways of diagnosing severe mental illnesses such as schizophrenia. Suffice it to say that a formal diagnosis may take some time to achieve, and that this time period may be extended where involved parties themselves delay the process because of underlying feelings about attached stigma.

Treatment

A student experiencing an episode of psychosis will most likely need to take 'time out' from studying. This is a point when universities may lose touch with the student because of a prolonged absence (as in the above vignette), and steps should be taken to monitor the situation with a view to re-engaging with the student to discuss studying possibilities during a period of wellness following psychosis. Most universities have in place procedures for 'suspending' (used here in a positive sense) a student's registration. Careful counselling may be required to ensure that the student is as aware as possible of time limits and other conditions tied to the suspension. As noted above, mental health professionals often take months to diagnose severe mental illness such as schizophrenia, and there can be reluctance to formally diagnose schizophrenia because of the associated stigma. Wherever possible universities need to take account of such periods of time and avoid penalizing students for things that are, often at least, out of their control.

Neuroleptic medications are often prescribed to manage the debilitating effects of the illness. Newer medications of this kind tend to have fewer side effects, and help with symptoms of hallucinations, muscle twitches (known as tardive dyskenisia) and lethargy. Talking treatments may also be used in conjunction with medication.

Detailed information about diagnosis, medications, side effects and talking treatments can be obtained from the Rethink National Advice Service. The Rethink National Advice Service is open by telephone, Monday to Friday 10.00 am to 3.00 pm. Full contact details including e-mail can be found at the end of this chapter.

> Although the majority of those diagnosed as having a severe mental illness will need to take some form of long-term medication, it is misleading to generalize about either the severity or the longevity of the illness. To take schizophrenia as an example: after a single episode accompanied by a diagnosis of the illness 25% of people will recover completely within 5 years, 50% will continue to display symptoms which fluctuate, often disappearing completely and then reoccurring over time; 15% will have severe, persistent problems and 10% will suffer life-long incapacity.
>
> (Rethink, 1995: 7)

Stigma

Stigma associated with mental illness is pervasive. Mental illness is perceived as something that happens to 'other' people. It is hard to comprehend for those with no basis in their own experience for interpreting the kind of difficulties being faced by the individual with the mental illness. Also it cannot be seen, though its manifestation in behaviours may of course be readily apparent. This lack of transparency, allied with the discomfort we all tend to feel when someone is acting in a way that is at odds with the social norms, perhaps underpins much of the stigma. In one sense at least, stigmatizing is a device for dealing with something one cannot see and cannot fathom, and which challenges one's preconceived notions of what is 'normal'. People tend to feel threatened by what they do not understand and feel they cannot control. Stigmatizing is one way of dealing with this threat. Unfortunately it has the effect of further lessening the chances of understanding, and may exacerbate tensions between the individual with the mental illness and those around him or her.

Sensational news reporting does not help to further understanding or generate balanced debate. In particular, news reporting often deals with very specific instances, yet uses general terms such as 'schizophrenic' in describing and analysing them. In this way news reports may serve to further distort rather than clarify common understandings. Stigma and discrimination are all around us in the language used in everyday speech, advertising, as well as other forms of communication. The fact that schizophrenia and other severe forms of mental illness are often treated as taboo subjects serves only to perpetuate misunderstanding of the conditions and misrepresentation of those who develop them.

Exercise

As an exercise, consider broadening your awareness of how language is used verbally, in print and broadcast media in relation to mental health and illness for a period of a week or two. You may be surprised by what you observe. My work with Rethink has involved travelling nationwide raising awareness, especially with students. Regularly I look out for an example of negative stereotyping or misrepresentation in news articles and adverts on the day I travel. I find this is a very useful way of bringing the issues surrounding severe mental illness to life. It can also act as a springboard for an exercise about forms of negative stereotyping and discrimination surrounding mental illness that the students may have read or heard but have not recognized as such.

Stigma will also contribute to how students who experience severe mental illness, and students generally, approach and use university welfare services and students' union services. Working with students' unions and others to enhance understanding in the student community is likely to be a practically useful way forward. I will return to this idea towards the end of the chapter.

Potential obstacles

Students are currently required to complete a UCAS form as part of the entry requirements for university on successful completion of preparatory studies. It is a useful indicator for institutions to gauge levels of support for prospective students. Students are encouraged to make known any disabilities and support needs to assist them with their studies. As discussed elsewhere in this book, it is unfortunate though understandable that some students with pre-existing mental illness withhold the information for fear of prejudicing their chances of obtaining a place, or of perceived reactions to their illness once at the university.

My discussions with welfare services staff at a handful of universities lead me to believe that only a small percentage of students with pre-existing mental illness difficulties make these difficulties known before enrolling. If this is the case, welfare services will find it a challenge to reach students with practical support in the early stages of studying, even if just to identify what is on offer. The likelihood of students' reluctance to disclose can be pre-empted with clear publicity materials outlining equal opportunities policies/statements around mental health and illness. In addition to this, students with pre-existing difficulties could be encouraged to make pre-entry contact to discuss support needs.

Access to welfare services is worth noting. Many universities operate satellite sites in addition to a main campus. Some courses may base students at satellite sites, and provide little reason for students to make use of the main site. If core welfare services are based around main sites, a regular periphery service reaching out to satellite sites is essential to keep all students and staff 'in the loop'. Students' unions can work along similar lines, targeting information and surgeries. Clearly, this is true of all the conditions and disabilities discussed in this book. In the case of mental illness, however, needs may not be predictable, and therefore regularity of available services becomes of crucial importance.

As indicated earlier, medications may affect students' ability to work to the best of their ability. Key things to be aware of include:

● lethargy, which may in turn affect concentration and retention of information;
● attendance at lectures and practical sessions may deteriorate;
● some students taking medications find it hard to motivate themselves in the mornings, and feel better able to attend and concentrate during afternoons.

If students recognize that they are experiencing difficulties with their coursework and/or mental health, they may feel the need to seek assistance. It is to be hoped that the university will have guidelines for referring and assisting students experiencing mental distress, including severe mental illness. In my experience of recent years, universities have found it increasingly difficult to assist students generally on a one-to-one basis, owing to a combination of factors including a rise in student numbers and strains on resources. It is clearly the case that universities need to try to ensure that support mechanisms on the ground are able to match the procedures and processes indicated in published guidelines and codes of practice.

Students experiencing severe mental illness difficulties will likely be caused further distress if they are turned away or made to feel that the person approached is not the 'right' person to talk to. The person approached (quite possibly a member of academic staff) may not feel they are the 'right' person to help the student, especially if the student appears to be in crisis. This is where an effective referral procedure and understanding of one's own university welfare service, counselling opportunities, and disability officer's roles are crucial for the student's well-being and member of staff's time management.

Coursework flexibility

Students who experience difficulties with their illness or medication may require some course or assignment flexibility.

> The appropriate boundaries between different kinds of support could be defined and included in a written statement to be discussed with each student as to what this may mean in practice. The support available and procedures for provision and access should be made as clear to students as possible. It would be helpful to have statements of general procedure which are discussed with students at the start of their studies along with their personal support plans. Although all plans are by nature provisional, it should make implementation of support simpler if a student has previously indicated how they feel possible problems are best dealt with and who, at what stage, should become involved.
>
> (Rethink, 1995: 17)

As far as those with a form of mental illness are concerned, modular teaching and credit accumulation coupled with a form of continual assessment may be an effective format of curriculum delivery. Traditional study and end of year exams are potentially difficult for students experiencing mental illness. If students change medication with uncomfortable side effects, or find it difficult to concentrate for periods, their ability to meet the course requirements at a crucial time may be hampered. They may have put in considerable effort at times when they are well enough to work, yet be unable to realize the fruits of that work at key examination times. Where modules and/or continual assessment provide opportunities to pass specific course modules that count towards the overall qualification, the student with a mental illness is advantaged by being able achieve something in a way that can be recorded and credited. A significant disruption to studies requires the student only to attempt a particular module or modules, rather than negotiate and contemplate the completion of an entire academic year's work.

Emergencies

It is relatively easy for a student to develop symptoms of severe mental illness without others noticing for some time. It is common for students to live in halls or shared housing, and in both situations it is possible for a student in distress to 'shut the door' on the world without friends or course colleagues being aware of serious difficulties. If this behaviour is prolonged, others will likely become concerned. A student developing symptoms of severe mental illness may be unaware that anything is wrong, and encouraging the person to seek help may not be practical. A fellow student may feel unable to resolve this problem and contacting a hall's crisis service/warden or university welfare services representative may be an appropriate way forward.

Universities are increasingly developing mental health and illness guidelines, and it may be useful for university welfare professionals and teaching staff to familiarize themselves with their institution's working groups and current procedures. Additionally, the Rethink *Students and Mental Health Resource Pack* (1995: 11, 12) outlines how an approach may be made to a student developing symptoms and staff accessing help. This may also be useful in informing the development of your institution's guidelines.

Mental health awareness

I have concentrated mainly on severe mental illness throughout the chapter but it is also important to understand mental health awareness: for everyone, students and staff. Each of us has mental health. I touched briefly on this earlier in the chapter:

> Perhaps it is useful to think of mental health as a continuum ranging from the relatively mild anxieties, disappointments and frustrations of everyday life to severe problems.
>
> (Rethink, 1995: 6)

Mental health is a part of our overall well-being, and yet we appear to spend a disproportionate amount of time and energy being aware of our mental health and ensuring we feel mentally healthy. A student lifestyle may at times be exhilarating, lonely, busy, stressful, relaxed, isolating, and demanding, physically, financially and emotionally. Many students without a diagnosis of mental illness or severe mental illness experience periods of low mood or despondency at some point while studying. These students probably will not develop a severe mental illness, but they will be experiencing fluctuations in their mental health.

A greater awareness of each individual's mental health, capacity for generating and dealing with stress, and wider understanding of mental illness will help to lessen the misunderstandings and stigma surrounding mental illness and severe mental illness. Universities can tackle the issues in an imaginative way by encouraging departments to work together along with the students' union and local voluntary agencies, such as Rethink and others.

The start of the academic year in early autumn is a prime time to promote awareness and dispel stigma. For first year students, the beginning of university can be disorientating. If your university colleagues need a 'reason' to promote awareness, a key date for your diary is 10 October, World Mental Health Day. World Mental Health Day can be the first step in your academic year calendar to reach all students and start to tackle difficult issues and misunderstandings, dispel stigma, and provide signposts to further help and assistance.

Reference

Rethink (1995) *The IRIS Project: Students and mental health resource pack*, Rethink, Surrey

This publication is out of print as the project has been adapted since 1995. A photocopy may be available from Rethink Publications (address below). Alternatively, a version may be available via the Rethink young people's Web site (see below).

Resources

Early Intervention: IRIS initiative to reduce the impact of schizophrenia IRIS have produced early intervention guidelines and a toolkit of practical use for mental health professionals. IRIS can be contacted at:

IRIS c/o Early Intervention Service
Harry Watton House, 97 Church Road
Aston, Birmingham B6 5UG
For background information and current updates surf the IRIS Web site:
www.iris–initiative.org.uk

Rethink: Severe Mental Illness

Rethink: Severe Mental Illness became the trading name of the National
Schizophrenia Fellowship in July 2002.

Rethink: Severe Mental Illness Advice Service
28 Castle Street, Kingston upon Thames
Surrey KT1 1SS
Monday–Friday 10.00 am to 3.00 pm
Tel: 020 8974 6814.
e–mail: info@rethink.org

Publications Department
Rethink
28 Castle Street
Kingston upon Thames
Surrey KT1 1SS

Rethink: Severe Mental Illness General Enquiries
Head Office, 30 Tabernacle Street
London EC2A 4DD
Tel: 0845 4560 455
Fax: 020 7330 9102
Web site: www.rethink.org

@ease Web site for young people

@ease is the mental health resource developed by Rethink. @ease is for all
young people, and especially those who may feel stressed or worried about
their thoughts and feelings. @ease aims to raise awareness of mental health
and illness, dispel stigma, and provide further sources of information and
support.
Web site: www.rethink.org/at-ease
e–mail: at-ease@rethink.org

13

Psychiatrically vulnerable students: stress, emotional disturbance

Mary Davies and Caralinda Jefferies

Introduction

The central issues of widening participation in higher education – the profile of student cohorts, entry routes and numbers of drop-outs – have brought to the forefront the urgent need to reflect on and develop strategies that are orientated towards student-centred learning. It is not the purpose of this chapter to debate the issues of pedagogy versus andragogy, except in so far as they are relevant to an understanding of how students learn. Widening participation has meant that lecturers and tutors are more likely to have to deal with issues surrounding those identified as 'psychologically vulnerable', and many feel ill-equipped to support students effectively.

Causes of vulnerability

The stress associated with studying at a higher level has been compounded in recent years by financial concerns which affect all sections of the student body, and although it is a recent phenomenon, it is in addition to the more traditional problems encountered. Many young undergraduates (those entering immediately after completion of studies at school or further education college) will be coping with the trauma of budgeting, time management, cooking and even laundry, for the first time. Many will have perceived themselves as 'big fish' in a little pond, and now they are the 'little fish', thus undermining their self-confidence. Some will be feeling isolated and unable to share their concerns with fellow students, most of whom are total strangers with an entirely different background, and often culture. Modern self-catering halls of residence organized into self-contained flatlets do not facilitate meeting a wide range of like-minded students with whom it would be possible to share problems. More traditional halls of residence with large common rooms and dining halls were better placed to provide this facility.

Students living at home, often to ease the financial burden, fare little better. Although family support may be present, past participation levels mean that few of these families will have a tradition of higher education and most are unable to provide the necessary breadth of support. In the authors' experience, students living at home are more likely to leave the campus immediately after lectures and will not attend on days when there are no classes, further increasing their isolation.

The rise in students in gainful employment to support the cost of their studies increases the trend to leave the campus and its support mechanisms; it reduces the student's opportunity to network, and creates additional problems for students already experiencing difficulties organizing their time. Research by Hilary Metcalf for the National Institute of Economic and Social Research (2001) confirms that 'students from poorer families are less likely to receive financial help from their families and are more likely to work in term time' and consequently 'working in term time means students have less time for study and academic achievement may suffer'. The study also showed that this is true where the parents do not possess degrees, therefore the students who require academic support the most may be the least likely to get it. Juggling time for lectures, study, work and socializing is a strain for all students; for those identified as 'psychologically vulnerable' it can be one stress too many.

Institutions, while working to assist students who need to earn money, are inadvertently adding to their problems. It is becoming more common to compact the academic week into two and a half to three days, and this tight schedule often means that students will have three consecutive lectures with no break. Students themselves are active promoters of this learning nightmare, often protesting at any gaps in their timetable, and will try their hardest to change the day of any lecture or tutorial delivered in isolation.

Many students identified as 'psychologically vulnerable' are adult returners. Although they will not generally be experiencing the stress of leaving home for the first time, and will normally have already developed time management skills, they will nevertheless bring into higher education problems of a different nature. Many of those who are guided into counselling and study support will tell the same story of a negative learning experience reinforced by messages that have consistently contradicted and undermined their belief in themselves as able learners. When these students enter higher education, the task of counsellors, study support tutors, and most crucially, their course tutors and lecturers, is to help them to, as one student has described it, 'unlearn the script' that has cast them as failures. Squires notes that adults often seem to internalize 'failure' and attribute it at least partly to themselves. And adult education itself is often compensatory, rather than continuing, sometimes having 'to demolish some bad construction work before it can begin again.' (Squires, 1997: 102). We can extend this metaphor into a consideration of the walls of protection that our students erect and which we, as lecturers and support tutors, need to be aware of since they so frequently form barriers between the student and their ability to learn, as we shall see in the case study below.

Janice's story

Janice's biography tells a story of silence as recourse in the face of those in authority, her teachers, who would not hear, and as defence against her peer group. She found safety in silence. Her experience links her as an adult to that of the 'silent' woman for whom 'speech is associated with acts of violence, and used without reason' (Gilligan, 1998: 69). Throughout her three years in higher education, Janice has cut herself off from language as a means of articulation and sharing of ideas, of engaging with her subject through discussion and debate.

We learn through language, through voicing our ideas. It is through language that we gain insight into ourselves, and that self-knowledge is as much a part of the learning experience for the student as knowledge of her subject. Mezirow talks about 'communicative learning', that is, 'learning to understand what others mean and to make ourselves understood' (Mezirow, 1998: 62). This form of learning is one which 'involves negotiation with others through language and gesture' (Mezirow, 1998: 36). The idea implies an ability to read others, to have a level of social skill that allows us to handle the dynamics of a group, in order for us to judge the balance of listening and response and be able to participate confidently.

Language, to have a voice, is empowerment; Janice's educational experience has been one of silence and disempowerment, which she has brought
with her into her present studies. She has silenced herself, unable to participate in tutorials while being painfully aware of tutors' perceptions of her as
inarticulate and non-participatory. From the tutors' point of view, of
course, they are unable to gauge or assess orally her level of knowledge and
engagement with the subject, which has ramifications for her associated
written assignments.

Janice came to study support to improve her writing skills. In an initial
needs assessment with her study support tutor, she had highlighted what
she saw as the discrepancy between her understanding of the content of her
subjects, and of the questions set in related assignments, and her inability to
translate that understanding into a coherent written form, to get down on
paper what was in her head. The problem was accentuated by some grammatical weaknesses. She is studying full time in a subject that has a heavy
content of reading and demands a high level of ability in use of language,
critical thinking and analysis. At the same time, she also has to contend with
the difficulties of supporting herself financially, and has a full-time job as a
coach driver which requires a commitment of five eight-hour shifts a week.
The job is demanding, with poor remuneration, which does not reflect the
high level of responsibility Janice holds.

In the last four years Janice has moved house five times. This follows a
pattern set during her childhood, when her father's army career took the
family on a number of moves across the country, disrupting her early school
years until the age of seven, when her parents divorced and Janice, her
mother and two younger brothers set up home in Wales. Janice recalls the
very great difficulties she had in integrating into her primary school, where
she was immediately singled out as different, 'not part of the club'. She had
an English accent and was very confused by Welsh language lessons, never
having heard a 'foreign language' talked in school before. Unlike her peers
she liked reading, and would frequently take books into class to absorb her
attention; she also wrote differently, and remembers that the children in her
class had never seen handwriting like hers before. The idea of difference was
set.

Another move took her to a different primary school for her last year,
unsure if she carried with her the headmaster's threat, following a fight with
a pupil ('my first fight in school'), that her 'reputation would follow her'. In
her new school Janice was immediately put into the remedial class, perhaps
because her records had not been transferred, but at 10 she had the strong
impression that the teachers did not know what to do with her. However,

she proved her ability by gobbling up the work set her, and was moved up to the top class.

The move to comprehensive school at 11 Janice described as a 'nightmare'. As in primary school, she was again singled out for her unusual surname, which dogged her all through school, and because she 'sounded English'. She recalls being picked on by her peer group for any mistake she made, and her 'difference' became marked in her teens: 'I hit puberty and got big.' Reading became a means of escape, and teachers noted that Janice would rather read than talk in a group.

Attempts by Janice to seek support and advice from her teachers were rebuffed. 'I felt that they were just saying, "This is how you deal with it; deal with it". I felt they should have stopped the bullying.' Janice began to miss school 'to get away from it', persuading her mother that she was ill, or missing the bus. Teachers noted that she was 'never in school' and unlikely to do well in her GCSEs. This was reflected in her grades, predominantly Ds, but achieving a B in Biology and a C in Chemistry, 'because I liked the teacher'.

There was some improvement in Janice's experience at a further education college, but it was still 'niggly' when she came across old classmates. Her subsequent educational path shows a strong determination and motivation to learn. After gaining her National Diploma in Science and Health Studies, she went on to university to study for a BA with Qualifying Teacher Status (QTS), completing the first two years in Science and Computing. She decided, on the advice of the course director, to change courses after being told by her tutor that she was 'no good', would 'never make a teacher' and 'don't come back'. She changed to a BSc in Biological Sciences and Educational Studies: 'I loved it.' She kept in contact with friends from the course in QTS, but failure in one exam and the death of her father got on top of her, and she did not complete her dissertation. 'I just gave up on it.'

Her mother persuaded Janice to return home after finding her a driving job. The living arrangements proved stressful, however, as she had to share a bed with her mother. After two months she moved out, rehoused by her local county council. During this time she completed a Level 1 course in British Sign Language then, finding herself bored, decided to follow up her interest in law, first stimulated by a module in Law in Education while studying for her QTS.

Janice described her confidence and self-esteem as 'not very well' when she took up her present place in higher education. She brought the pattern of silence with her, unable to talk in tutorials or seminars, afraid of making a mistake, of getting picked on. 'I feel too scared to ask because I don't want to be shown up.' Now in her third year, Janice is still wary of her student circle and doesn't get asked to socialize with them. She describes her social skills as 'not brilliant' and finds that this hampers her ability to interact with other students. She feels strongly that her fear of talking has affected her ability to learn. 'I find it difficult to talk about assignments because I try to deflect taunts.'

Her relationship with her tutors and lecturers she describes as generally good. 'They take the mickey out of us, but it's not nasty.' She is able to respond best to one particular lecturer who uses humour to draw her out to answer a question. Direct questions, like 'Do you have any opinion?' or 'Do you have a point of view?' throw her, and in this, her final year, she feels vulnerable since the make-up of the group has changed. In the previous group, she chose to sit beside a bright student, quick to answer, who shielded her from exposure. She feels that now she has to fend for herself, and tries to shrink behind other people who are keen to go forward.

In response to one tutor's method of asking students to answer questions off a sheet, she explained that she scans the answers at the bottom and gives him what he wants to hear to 'ward off attack. I'm warding him off with a stick.' Janice feels strongly that she would have liked the opportunity to explain her difficulties to her tutors. This has had implications for her written work, 'I feel too shy to ask for help with my assignments. I'm too scared to say anything just in case they think me stupid or something. I don't want to be different. Not after school.'

Student-centred learning

It is clear that Janice's past experience has been one of not being heard, of difference as stigma and silence as refuge and defence. Her account also suggests a perception of the teacher as authority, thus, in andragogical terms, placing the teacher rather than the student at the centre of learning. 'The teacher teaches and the students are taught; the teacher knows everything and the students know nothing; the teacher thinks and the students are thought about' (Freire, 1990: 239). Student-centred learning uses the student's past or recalled experiences to facilitate learning by encouraging reflection on those past experiences. Knowles (1998) links this to the idea of moving from being a dependent personality to a self-directing one: that is, one that is goal-orientated, activity-orientated and learning-orientated.

These are the motivations that often attract adults back into learning (Jarvis, Holford and Griffin, 1998: 78), but they may also choose for their subject one that is studied through a pedagogical approach to learning, and that demands teacher-centred methods of delivery, 'making learners learn what they were being taught by their teachers' (Houle, 1998: 62). This is education conceived as the transmission of a fixed content, Freire's '"banking" concept of education': the student receives 'deposits' of knowledge from the teacher; 'the scope of the action allowed to the student extends only as far as receiving, filing and storing the deposits' (Freire, 1997: 144–45). In this context, learners are passive receptacles rather than active participants in their own learning. It is a problem that tutors, lecturers and support staff need to be aware of and address in encouraging self-directed learning, to give students a say in the learning process.

Adult students are often aware of their own difficulties and, like Janice, will approach study support tutors to help them direct their studies. If we extend the idea of self-directed learning into the broader sense of helping students find out how they learn, then there is much subject tutors can do to give students such as Janice a say in the learning process. For the study support tutor, identifying students' learning needs and enabling them to voice those needs is the first step in devising a learning programme with individual students. It is a process in which the subject tutor can not only participate, but also initiate.

Assessment of needs

A needs assessment takes account of the experiences students bring with them into their learning environment, and uses the learning biography to help students create their learning profile. From this, students are encouraged to diagnose their educational needs and to identify, through their own assessment, their level of ability in skills they already have. Even within a lecture, students can be encouraged to be aware of skills development through, for example, a set of simple strategies as set out below.

Discussing the learning process

Explain:

- which skills you are hoping to develop within the context of the subject;

- what information or skill you are expecting the students to learn;
- the relationship to other learning experiences.

Discuss learning strategies:

- encourage students to explore which strategies work for them;
- facilitate a 'share' session of strategies that have been successful and that optimize their learning strengths;
- encourage students to analyse why certain strategies work and others do not (Krupska and Klein, 1995: resource sheet 8).

We should also be aware that students who have underdeveloped skills in the area of, for example, written work may have strong life skills that they can apply when they direct their own learning. It is clear in Janice's case that, in juggling her studying with her full-time job, Janice's time management and organizational skills are very strong; and her determination to advance her studies, despite the poverty of her experience in secondary school and later rejection at higher education level, indicates a resilience and high level of determination to overcome the social obstacles to her learning. She also had some knowledge and experience of her subject from her course in QTS, and her reading skills are very strong.

According to Freire's thinking, 'Everyone enters every learning situation with more or less articulate ideas about the topic at hand' (cited in Kolb, 1997: 145). In those students who are able to express those ideas, tutors and lecturers can more easily identify and assess levels of the essential skills the higher education student needs to develop in order to succeed. Brookfield (1998: 60) identifies five key skills areas:

- critical thinking;
- recognizing and challenging assumptions;
- challenging the importance of the context;
- being willing to explore alternatives;
- becoming reflectively sceptical.

These are skills that students apply in their writing, but their development begins through questioning in discussion and debate. For students such as Janice, who are unable to enter this arena, the initial needs assessment with a tutor can offer a safe environment in which the student can begin to articulate his/her experience and to engage with the subject through talk. In this situation, the role of the tutor becomes that of facilitator, and can be extended into group sessions that facilitate peer learning, where students are encouraged to share their biographies and can benefit and learn from each other's experience. It offers, too, an opportunity for the teacher to listen to the language students use in talking about their experiences, which can provide a vital clue to the identification of students' vulnerabilities.

Gremmo and Abe (1997: 194) base their study of the role of the teacher in learning on the premise that 'it is really the learner who is the essential component in any pedagogical event'. By listening to students, by helping them to identify and articulate their needs, we can go some way towards putting students at the centre of their learning experience. Where the subject tutor is the first point of contact in a needs assessment, that tutor must be able to offer guidance based on his or her understanding of the student's needs as practical or emotional. Of course in practice, as in Janice's case, the two are interlinked, and in the scenario that facilitates a dialogue between tutor and student, the next step is to open the channels of communication between subject tutor, study support tutor and counsellor, to negotiate with the student a network of support that addresses the whole person.

The work Janice has done with her counsellor and study support tutor has raised her confidence to the point where she is able to answer tentatively when asked for opinions by tutors, and is able to respond in discussions with her peer group when she is certain of her knowledge. But the third element of support, from her tutors, is not in place because they do not have knowledge of her learning difficulties, which are based on complex emotional and psychological factors.

Janice's case highlights the difficulties for tutors and lecturers in identifying students who are vulnerable, who as a result may drop out or fail a course, and who will almost certainly have a rate of achievement below their ability and probably their expectations. It is this disjuncture between the student's level of ability and actual result that has a strongly negative and detrimental affect on motivation and determination to succeed. Based on her academic background in further and higher education, her prior knowledge of and real enthusiasm for her subject, Janice expected to do well, but she found instead that past experiences continued to intrude and effectively block her progress. Similarly, her tutors know her as a hard worker who hands in assignments on time and has a high attendance record, but in tutorials she is perceived as passive and non-participatory. Knowledge of students' expectations of themselves, based on their experience and level of skill, can help tutors and lecturers recognize a warning bell which they must act on, the discrepancy between the appearance of attitudes such as Janice shows in a seminar, and the actual expectation of success that may have been raised in the self-assessment.

Strategic planning for learning

Although Janice is a mature student with many of the problems associated with adult returners, the support mechanisms required for her support are equally valid for all vulnerable students. It is recognized that stress can have psychophysiological effects. Higher education providers must recognize this, and consider solutions at a strategic level. The problems of these students will not disappear and in the current climate their numbers will be on the increase.

Trained counsellors and study support tutors are essential elements in providing support for these students. Many of the problems encountered by students can be eased by correct diagnosis and the installation of a recovery programme, but teamwork is essential and, while confidentiality is paramount, counsellors cannot work in isolation. They must enlist the support of programme directors, year tutors and/or personal tutors. Teaching staff do not need to know details, and indeed issues of confidentiality govern what and how much information can be given out to staff, but an awareness that there is a problem and that it is being dealt with is helpful, and can assist the academic staff in being constructive rather than being – albeit inadvertently – destructive. It is therefore vital that there is two-way communication between tutors/lecturers and counsellors. Counsellors – and also study support tutors – can act as mediators between students and their tutors, and where tutors guide their students towards counselling, this in itself will help students to see them as open to their needs. They will then be encouraged to place more confidence in revealing problems to subject staff.

Lecturers and tutors are not trained counsellors, and cannot necessarily be expected to provide the individual support needed. However, as Janice's case demonstrates, tutors and lecturers need to make themselves aware of the signs of stress, which can be indicators of a deeper difficulty. Students who seek guidance through study support and counselling often have one or more of the following problems:

- Poor time management/organizational skills, which may result in:
  - poor attendance;

- consistently missed deadlines;
- an inability to complete an assignment.
- Procrastination, often from fear of tackling an assignment.
- Low level of concentration in seminars/tutorials.
- Difficulty in assimilating and processing information, for example from hand-outs/texts under discussion.
- Shyness, reticence, unwillingness to participate in group discussions.
- Underdeveloped, immature social skills (poor mixer; difficulty in relating to peers).

Some of these are general difficulties that many students experience as a matter of course in adjusting to independent study in higher education, and this is where close liaison with support staff is essential in ensuring the early identification of students whose learning difficulties may have their root in an inner vulnerability. A programme of staff development can provide tutors and lecturers with useful guidelines on the typical symptoms associated with the more common disorders, such as depression, obsessive compulsive disorder, mania, eating disorders, self-harm, and phobias. Academic staff need to be aware of the support available and the mechanisms to trigger that support. Sometimes staff feel that a student with a problem has a problem with them, unaware that their colleagues are thinking the same thing. Greater awareness of psychological disorders and the way they manifest themselves in student behaviour and learning patterns is an invaluable tool.

All staff have a responsibility towards their students. These students will not go away; they have been accepted onto a programme of study, and they may have made great sacrifices to join. Teaching staff have a role to play, and can often easily provide valued support. Induction is a key time for many vulnerable students, setting the scene for the next three years. A welcoming environment that recognizes individuals, rather than treating students as a 'mass onslaught', is helpful, as is a social event such as a cheese and wine reception where staff/student barriers are broken down. A brief chat can often allay fears and reduce stress before it gets beyond a student's control and begins to require professional help.

Students need to be fully aware of the support mechanisms that are available, and how to access them. A pile of material delivered in the post in the summer prior to first enrolment or during induction is often lost. During this time students are being inundated with information, and it can be more beneficial for counsellors to be introduced to groups of students a little after induction.

Staff need to be aware of the damaging effects of student isolation within a group. The rejection of peers is sometimes passively condoned by staff, as to tackle the problem appears to be a task beyond their skills, and not considered by some to be in their remit. As noted in Janice's case, it is possible to develop a strategy to tackle the problem from the perspective of both the isolated student and the group as a whole.

In another case met by the author, a mature student with severe personal hygiene problems was given a wide berth by students (and teaching staff). Referral to the student counsellor did not have the desired effect. The stress of his isolation appeared to trigger antisocial behaviour such as knuckle biting and grunting noises in class. When a student in the group was persuaded to discuss the hygiene problem with him, his first question was 'Is that why nobody sits with me?' There were logistical problems that did not allow him to bathe regularly; these were discussed and a solution acceptable to the group was found. The hygiene problem improved, and gradually the antisocial behaviour diminished. The student, while never becoming the most popular member of the group, at least became a participating member and successfully completed his studies. The group awareness of his problems was also noticeable, and improved group cohesion generally. He was accepted.

Early diagnosis of shortfalls in study skills can assist in diminishing the stress associated with study at higher level, but it needs to be followed up by a structured programme of study support, and should be a routine part of the early months of study. Identification in the first examination board is often too late, as a pattern of failure has begun, often reinforcing past failure (as in Janice's case), and the student may already have opted out of the experience. An opportunity has been wasted.

Traditional higher education teaching styles do not encourage group cohesion, or expect a high level of study skills development. Staff development is needed to encourage staff to understand the nature of the study skills deficiencies, and to develop a means of embedding their development throughout the curriculum and in the assessment strategies employed. As far as the latter is concerned, course design and structure may not allow for flexibility where the assessment contributes to the final grade. However where there is flexibility within course work, students can benefit from a variety of assessment tasks that allow them to demonstrate their knowledge through methods that play to their strengths.

The work going on in colleges of further education in working with students' learning styles is now being taken on board by higher education institutions. In particular, the holistic approaches to learning taken by support tutors in working with dyslexic students also benefit non-dyslexic students: dyslexia friendly teaching is good for all. Such strategies recognize that students have individual cognitive styles, thus students with strong visual/spatial skills would benefit from the opportunity of demonstrating their knowledge through a presentation which allows them to use visual aids such as posters, slides, OHPs, or software packages such as PowerPoint. By helping students to identify and optimize their own learning strengths, we can actively encourage them to 'take charge of their own learning'. Krupska and Klein, (1995: resource sheet 8) suggest a number of strategies to help students do this:

● Offer a variety of methods and approaches for them to select or discover which works best for them.
● Set up active learning situations where they can explain or demonstrate things to each other, work in pairs or groups, select activities or projects, set goals.
● Stress self-checking and give plenty of opportunity for self-assessment.

Similarly, lecturers can build holistic teaching strategies into their delivery of subject matter:

● Introduce the 'whole picture' and then the parts within it.
● Make explicit links from particular examples to the general overall idea.
● Give concrete examples (using audio-visual aids or demonstrations where possible) to build up a 'picture' of abstract ideas.

Conclusion

Subject tutors and lecturers can exploit the links with study support and dyslexia support tutors, to work with them in developing teaching and learning strategies that are orientated towards student learning styles. This gives students an experience of education that helps them to see themselves as individual learners, and in many cases will encourage them towards a perception of themselves as learners who can succeed. This is often the greatest challenge for both subject and support staff. There are many students in mainstream education like Janice, who are unable to articulate their needs, and who are not heard. By putting students at the centre of learning, we give them a voice.

References

Brookfield, S (1998) Developing critical thinkers: challenging adults to explore alternative ways of thinking and acting, in *The Theory and Practice of Learning*, ed P Jarvis, J Holford and C Griffin, Kogan Page, London

Freire, P (1990) Pedagogy of the oppressed, in *The Adult Learner: A neglected species*, ed M Knowles, Gulf Publishing, Houston, Texas

Freire, P (1997) Education for critical consciousness, in *Culture and Processes of Adult Learning*, ed M Thorpe, R Edwards and A Hanson, Routledge, London

Gilligan, C (1998) In a different voice, in *The Theory and Practice of Learning*, ed P Jarvis, J Holford and C Griffin, Kogan Page, London

Gemmo, M J and Abe, D (1997) Teaching learning: redefining the teacher's role, in *Culture and Processes of Adult Learning*, ed M Thorpe, R Edwards and A Hanson, Routledge, London

Houle, C O (1998) Self-directed learning, in *The Theory and Practice of Learning*, ed P Jarvis, J Holford and C Griffin, Kogan Page, London

Jarvis, P, Holford, J and Griffin, C (1998) *The Theory and Practice of Learning*, Kogan Page, London

Knowles, M (1998) The modern practice of adult education, in *The Theory and Practice of Learning*, ed P Jarvis, J Holford and C Griffin, Kogan Page, London

Kolb, D A (1997) The process of experiential learning, in *Culture and Processes of Adult Learning*, ed M Thorpe, R Edwards and A Hanson, Routledge, London

Krupska, M and Klein, C (1995) *Demystifying Dyslexia*, London Language and Literacy Unit, Southwark College, London

Metcalf, H (2001) Discussion Paper 186, National Institute of Social and Economic Research, London (October)

Mezirow, J (1998) Transformative dimensions of adult learning, in *The Theory and Practice of Learning*, ed P Jarvis, J Holford and C Griffin, Kogan Page, London

Squires, G (1997) Education for adults, in *Culture and Processes of Adult Learning*, ed M Thorpe, R Edwards and A Hanson, Routledge, London

14

Issues for pedagogy (3)

Stuart Powell

The changing face of university life

Davies and Jefferies summarize in their chapter the many changes that have taken place in the HE sector over recent years. Widening participation has meant that many students are the first in their families to have the opportunity to go to university. At the same time the increased cost of being a student means that many more students live at home and attend their local university than was the case previously, and many more now try to support themselves financially by undertaking paid employment at the same time as their studies.

Universities themselves have changed also. Davies and Jefferies note a trend towards compacting the academic week, thus bringing new stresses of crammed timetables interspersed with periods of possible isolation, particularly for those living at home. Wade notes the ubiquitous presence of satellite campuses and the tendency to locate core welfare services centrally. In all of this there are clearly different, if not increased, possibilities for psychological stress. Wade makes similar points to Davies and Jefferies about the stresses that can be caused directly by universities, where setting challenges for students is a deliberate intention of programmes of study. He goes on to note that the kinds of difficulty in coping with stress that students experience may develop into mental illness.

University educators therefore need to recognize that these new pressures exist, and try to find new ways of offering support. Most teachers at all levels of the educational system will vouch for the debilitating effect of new pressures on learners. Any notion of 'special teaching' will need to encompass the capability of responding proactively to changing social and economic circumstances. Ideas from Davies and Jefferies such as 'unlearning the script' would seem to be useful parts of any such capability.

Difficulty of identification

Davies and Jefferies highlight the difficulty for tutors in identifying 'vulnerability', and clearly there are always going to be problems in identifying something that has not yet manifested itself. These authors offer guidance for tutors, for example in noting discrepancies between the student's attitudes in seminars and their 'actual expectations of success' raised in self-assessment, and types of persistent procrastination, often from fear of tackling an assignment.

In the case of severe mental illness, as Wade describes, the illness can 'strike young people at any time'. Wade notes that the young man in his vignette had shown no signs of predisposition to mental illness during his first years at university. It was only in his final year that he experienced psychosis. University educators can therefore take nothing for granted when it comes to judging the mental health of students and indeed staff. They need to remain aware that changes can occur within the individual at any time, and they need to be ready to try to respond appropriately.

Indeed, in remaining aware, tutors need to recognize that one feature of behaviour may be indicative of a different, though related problem. For example, Davies and Jefferies note that stress can have psychophysiological effects. Similarly Wade notes lethargy as one indicator of the effects of medication. What the lecturer sees therefore is a physiological phenomenon, but the root of the student's experience is the psychological stress of the situation, or in the latter example above, the medication taken to alleviate stress. Such effects may therefore be the first indicators of a problem, and thus need careful interpretation by tutors.

The importance of teamwork

Special teaching cannot be conceived of as something that can be operated in isolation. Davies and Jefferies note that teamwork is essential. They suggest that support staff need to act as mediators between students and their tutors, and clearly academic staff need to cooperate if strategies are to be consistent enough to have a chance of success. Such cooperation may be made harder as HEIs move towards more modular forms of curriculum delivery, and as a result the strengthening of links between personal tutors, support staff and general academic staff is crucial. In short, the more compartmentalized a student's programme becomes, the more clear the lines of communication need to be. It is also the case that these lines need to be transparent: that is, known to and available for the student him/herself.

Stigma

Wade discusses the stigma that is often associated with mental illness. What he describes applies to many of the other conditions covered in this book, though perhaps to a lesser extent. He is right to suggest that stigmatizing is a way of dealing with something that is threatening, in this case to one's understanding of people and one's preconceptions of 'normal' behaviour. Lecturers need to be aware of the way in which stigmatizing can lead to further problems, by exacerbating tensions between the individual student and others around him or her. They also need to act to inhibit any tendency of their own to stereotype, and to offer information to all concerned so that the ignorance that often underpins stigma is diminished. It may be that a lecturer needs to attend to group understandings of issues by the kind of exercise discussed by Wade, looking in print and broadcast media for examples of stereotyping and misrepresentation. Special teaching may require that time is taken out from the regular curriculum in order to deal with issues surrounding individuals, recognizing, of course, their need for approval and involvement in such activities.

The significance of self-esteem

In the vignette given by Davies and Jefferies, the trials and tribulations of Janice within formal education and beyond underscore the significance of self-esteem in an individual's development. To most educators this significance is self-evident, and certainly teachers within the school sector would use the concept in their ways of approaching children's learning as a part of common practice. Students entering university will have a developed sense of their own worth in academic terms. Clearly, they will also have a sense of self-worth in non-academic skills, in the social arena and so on. Self-esteem is best understood as a variable within an individual that is influenced by context, rather than as a global feature of someone's persona, though clearly one aspect can begin to dominate all others: for example, the student who begins to achieve poorly in mathematics may begin to doubt his/her ability in all other subjects encountered.

At university entrance, a sense of self-worth (at whatever level) may be well established in the individual. Nevertheless, at this stage levels of self-esteem may be challenged in a way never before experienced by the student. A seemingly robust sense of self-identity and self-worth can become fractured. 'Special teaching' requires therefore that students particularly at risk of psychological strain, in the way described by Wade and by Davies and Jefferies, are identified, and the kinds of strategy described by these authors are put into place by way of support. It requires that for some individual students, where necessary, enhancing self-esteem is given precedence over more traditional markers of academic success.

Clearly, in the vignette used by Davies and Jefferies, Janice needs to be successful at her academic studies in order for her esteem to be enhanced, and I am not suggesting here that attaining such success should be ignored. Rather I am suggesting that direct efforts need to be focused on enhancing her self-esteem as an educational priority amongst others. The issues around student-centred learning discussed by Davies and Jefferies would form a part of that focusing. Many students in similar positions to Janice need to be enabled to move from dependency to self-direction. Enabling a student to reflect on his/her own progress, in personal terms outside of formal assessment procedures, would form another part of that focusing.

Afterword

Stuart Powell

Having brought together a range of topics and tried to connect them into unifying themes, I remain aware of the difficulties of laying down principles for an effective pedagogy that will apply across curriculum areas for all students. I am also aware that the range of topics addressed in this book will necessarily exclude some groups of students and some situations in which higher education teaching will, in one sense or another, need to be special. I suggest that this does not render the enterprise of this book wasted, but rather perhaps incomplete. Certainly, the range of situations requiring special teaching of one kind or another is likely to expand over future years as the changes noted in the main body of the text of this book take effect. For those of us who want to pursue an agenda of widening participation and an inclusive approach to the education of all students, the opportunities for testing our ingenuity and commitment are considerable.

I note also that on many occasions I have suggested that academic staff need to be made aware of various issues, and it does seem to me that, accepting all the specific guidance given by colleagues and the strategies for successful inclusion, a central need is for the general awareness of all academic colleagues to be raised. It is clearly not enough for support staff to have knowledge of special learning needs, skill in curriculum adaptation and alternative modes of delivery and attitudes that are likely to enhance the prospects for inclusion for all, if they find themselves operating in isolation of their colleagues. In short, all staff should have defined access to these things. Planners and curriculum organizers, as well as those who deliver the teaching, need to be aware at least of the issues, and be prepared to seek advice and guidance where necessary. The pervasive intention to include the needs of all students in the whole of the process of curriculum design and planning as well as delivery, combined with an ability to ask appropriate questions in order to ensure inclusion, are perhaps the main necessary prerequisites for success.

Of course all of this requires effort as well as intention, and here I am reminded of an individual with autism who pointed out (and I paraphrase): 'If I am the one with all the social problems and the one who can't understand what other people are thinking and wanting me to do – if I am the one who has lots of problems in getting to learn things – then why is it always me who has to make all the effort?'

Index